<u>Martial Arts without a Mouth:</u>

<u>Martial Arts Philosophy</u>

<u>By: Shifu Daniel Schultz</u>

Table of Contents

Introduction

The inspiration for this book started from a place one couldn't call orthodox. My teacher posted a picture of himself practicing Kung fu and edited the picture's color and contrast in a way that resulted in his mouth disappearing. One of my senior Kung fu brothers commented on the photo saying, "Kung fu without a mouth!" At first I took it as a funny joke and nothing more, but the more I thought about it the more I realized there was wisdom in those words as well.

Oftentimes we get in our own way along our journeys and one of the most common ways it is done is through our mouths. Speaking and giving opinions during times we should be learning and listening. If we are speaking, we are not listening. Thus we miss many potential lessons. Humans often tend to get so caught up in themselves that they stunt their growth for many years to even the end of their lives. With the way we use our mouths, it might be better if we had no mouths at all.

So this inspired me to write about martial philosophies and the traps along the way of life. And yes I do acknowledge the irony of writing a book to talk about being quiet and listening, but perhaps we'll all learn something through this together, so I will continue writing for now.

The way I plan to organize this book is to first talk about problems, traps, and mistakes that lead to stunted growth. Then the next section will talk of remedying such mistakes. The next two sections after that will be talking from the perspectives of two major schools of thought, both Buddhism and Daoism. While Buddhism and Daoism are primarily ways of thinking there are also sects of each that incorporate religious aspects into it. But that is not where this book goes. This book talks of these topics as what they primarily are, a way to look at and understand reality. Basically philosophy. The reason why I include them in a book about martial arts philosophy, while I don't see them as necessary to study martial arts, many martial arts were created and developed by those who studied these ideologies. I have found that studying these ways of thought gave a lot of insight into these arts and a lot of understanding as to how and why things developed in certain ways. So while not necessary to learn martial arts, the two are intertwined. One informs the other and that is why I include them. The last section will be for final thoughts.

It is my sincere hope that this book will be of benefit to those who read it. Train hard, think deeply, but listen more than you speak.

Wu De

The only way to properly start this book I believe is to bring up the topic of Wu De. As philosophy and morality are intrinsically linked. Wu De literally means Martial Virtue. It is essentially a code of morality linked to martial arts. Before guns existed, martial arts training was a great equalizer. If you were well trained in martial arts, you had a lot of power within your hands. So Wu De was essentially a morality code to keep ourselves in line. Knowing that you hold the power of life and death in your hands means that we hold equal responsibility not only to help others, but to keep ourselves in line to not take advantage of others weaknesses.

This code can be divided into two parts for discussion. There is external morality and internal morality. In other words, how you act on the outside and who you are on the inside. The body and mind.

For external morality it can be explained in five parts. Humility, Trust, Respect, Loyalty, and Righteousness. Humility is the water that douses the fire of our own ego. With growth in skills it is easy to fall into the traps of the ego. Instead of puffing up oneself one should use their skills to lift others. Others may put us on a pedestal, but we must step down and remind ourselves that we are no different from those around us. We are all equals and we all go through similar hardships, so we must remember to keep humble.

We must learn to trust others and we must show it with our actions. This does not mean blind faith. Rather we must not assume betrayal without reason. Without trust, there cannot be a relationship, for a relationship without trust is not a relationship.

Respect is the foundation for compassion and love. In order to love, there must be mutual acceptance. Respect is the understanding that though we may be different from others, we are the same. Though they may see things differently, they are still like us. Respect is the acceptance of this.

When we have power over others, it is important to remember loyalty. Perhaps we may be in a high position, but we didn't get there alone. Others have been there to raise us, care for us, laugh with us, cry with us. When one forgets this, they betray their upbringing. Instead we must use whatever power we have to lift up those that helped us.

With power we need righteousness. We must pursue what is right, right wrongs, and use what we have for others. Not to line our pockets. With power many pursue selfish gains in hopes that they will find happiness. Though they are selfish, have compassion for them as they are suffering. We must pursue what is right and use our power for others. Using power for ourselves leaves us empty and alone. But everyone using it for others provides community. We must also remember that in the pursuit of righteousness, it is easy to become self-righteous. What is righteous in one scenario may be completely wrong in another. Which is why we must continue to search for righteousness as anyone who claims to be righteous is far from it and breaks the previous rules of remaining humble and having respect.

Now we move on to internal morality. Internal morality is what you think, believe, intend on the inside that might not be visible on the outside. These are Will, Endurance, Perseverance, Patience, and Courage. We must have a strong willpower to do what is right even when it is difficult. We must Endure and persevere in order to help others and show compassion in a world where there are many things that hurt us. We must be patient and understand that those who lash out do so out of fear of insecurities. We must be courageous enough to walk the path of compassion. Even if we walk it alone. Internal morality, the mind, the intent, is the driving force behind external morality.

I like to interpret the two as action (external) and intent (internal). Everyone has heard the phrase, "actions speak louder than words." But I would say it is not quite correct. It is putting the external morality above internal morality when in reality they are not meant to be separate things but reflections of the same. I would instead say, "Intent and words without actions are empty. Actions with wrong intent are selfish. Intent coinciding with actions is true morality." One cannot truly exist without the other. If one talks of all the things that would be right, but does nothing to make it so, then it brings attention to the issue, but work isn't done to correct it. If one does good deeds, but his intent is selfish, then good things are done, but they are done to fuel greed or pride. One man can feed the homeless to make himself look like a good person, thus selfish intentions behind his act. Another can say, "we should feed the homeless," and yet do nothing about it. Both people are half correct, yet that means they are also half wrong. When one's intentions match their actions, then they have true morality.

To summarize, Wu De is a code of ethics to keep one in check. It serves to kill our egos and to properly interact with others. To replace ego with compassion and love. To keep us moving forward and doing the right thing even during trying times. It is the water to douse our fire and keep us from getting out of control. When falling into ego traps, we must keep this way in our mind and hearts.

Training Poisons and Traps

Lineage wars

To start off this list of ego traps, let us talk about lineage. In martial arts, lineage is a heated topic. Before lineage was kept as a way of honoring the ancestors who passed these arts down the line. As they ended up in our hands as a result of their hard work, it is important to acknowledge and respect the work they did. In many kung fu schools there would be pictures on the wall of past masters and even perhaps an ancestral altar being a place that one would acknowledge and pay respects to them.

In time, lineage would then eventually be used as a way to measure the credibility of a martial artist. If one had a well tracked and credible lineage, then it would be taken as evidence that the current martial artist in question was credible. In one way this is good, as it is a way to weed out scam artists who make false claims, but it has become a much more toxic discussion as now lineage has become the "proof" of your skills.

The thing is lineage is important, but it is not everything. There are many people who have a credible lineage, yet their skills are poor. And there are many who either have a non-famous lineage or a poorly tracked lineage, yet their skills are profound.

Lineage alone cannot be used as proof. The need to "prove" through lineage has also spawned many people who define their entire selves through their lineage and never do anything for themselves.

Another reason that lineage proving became so popular is because of cultural context. In China, there is a heavy influence of cultural utopianism. Utopianism is defined as, "the belief in or pursuit of a state in which everything is perfect, typically regarded as unrealistic or idealistic." With this in mind and the fact that China takes great pride in being one of the oldest recorded cultures in the world, let's now look at some historical claims.

Taijiquan is a martial art whose historical claims are still argued today. The claim that I believe is that Taijiquan was created in the 1600s at Chen village. But there is a claim that it was created in the 1200s by Zhang Senfeng. The story goes that Zhang had studied martial arts at Shaolin, but then created Taijiquan after becoming inspired by a battle of survival between a snake and a crane. Then brought the art to Wudang and from there eventually spread to Chen village. Not only is there no evidence that this historical claim is accurate, but there is more proof that the previous claim is more accurate. Zhang Senfeng was credited as the writer of the Dao De Jing and eventually he was considered to be immortal. There is no evidence that Zhang was related to martial practice. There is also some evidence that Zhang SenFeng's name was used as a cover up for some royal politics in order to cover up assassination attempts of those in line for the throne, but I think I will leave more of the specifics to those more qualified to speak of them then myself and move on.

Keeping the previous claims in mind, the story of an immortal creating this well known system upon inspiration from this tale is much more of an inspiring and pretty story than the previous claim. And the older time frame gives much more credibility than the Chen story, especially as we consider the, "older is better," part of the culture. If something is older, it is looked at as more credible as it is time tested. We also must consider one more cultural aspect. Claiming for example to have created your own style is considered incredibly rude as part of the culture teaches that one must stay humble.

So many claims of style's origins were embellished into legends as people wanted to not only give themselves credibility in lineage, but not to come off rude. So many stories of systems being created typically start with involvement of immortals, monks, or famous historical figures being the origins of the art. To be fair, it sounds a lot better than, "I made it up in my backyard." But this all gives us more context for why lineage credibility is held in such high regard. It became permeated into the culture to the point where many treat it as a means of credibility instead of a way to respect those that came before us.

We can see through all this why it is an ego trap. When one defines people's entire existence through lineage, it creates a toxic environment where lineage is used as a pecking order. Those with well-known lineage stand above those that don't. My teacher's teacher in the Ma family arts was once asked about his lineage during his class. Instead of giving an answer like many would, he turned to the student and raised his hands. He then said, "Here it is. My lineage is in my hands. You want to know my lineage, let's cross hands." Lineage is not proof of skills. Having a decent lineage does not guarantee that you will have good skills. There are many possible hiccups along the transition. Maybe the teacher was good skill wise, but maybe he sucked at teaching. Maybe the student didn't work hard or wasn't ready to study with this teacher. One must be ready physically and mentally and work hard. Then the teacher-student relationship must be cultivated. There are many factors to consider in whether a practitioner will be skillful. But in the end there is only one way to prove skill and that is putting ourselves to the test.

Having a good lineage gives us a good chance of obtaining skills, but it is not the only factor. Getting too caught in lineage can turn us into petty egotistical people. This ego trip will only serve to shut our minds to the lessons around us and stunt our growth and chances to learn. People without famous lineages have good things to say too. In fact, some of the best martial artists with the most profound things to say that I met had very little to say in regard to lineage. And in contrast some who had great lineages and held them with pride I found to be of little skill. Lineage shouldn't be a badge of honor. Lineage shouldn't be bastardized in such a way. Martial lineage is meant to be a way to pay respects. Put in simple terms, be thankful to your grandparents. They took a turn in shaping who you are. Don't shame their names by using them for selfish gain. Bring lineage to a place of respect, or it will forever bind you and prevent you from walking the path.

The Ego Lies and Flatters

My teacher has told me before to never buy my own headlines. Among the many ego traps there are along the journey, perhaps one of the biggest is believing ourselves to be experts. Whether we realize it or not, doing so is a quick way to stop learning and growing. We may even think consciously that we have much to learn, but our subconscious has already shut out other opportunities to learn. If we were responsible for creating a newspaper, then we would be responsible for what is put in that newspaper. Next day we go out and buy a newspaper. It's the one we wrote. We read it. But since we wrote it, we gained nothing from it that we didn't already know. This is what it is like to fall into this ego trap.

For many, they seek validation. Once we begin to obtain skills and knowledge, we are tempted to become enamored by ourselves for what we've done. But this is a slippery slope not easily escapable. People become complacent with what they know and lose the drive to learn more. The natural state of reality is constant change and growth. This kind of attitude fights the natural state of things and creates an unhealthy, closed off mind. No matter the amount we learn in our life, it will never be more than a spec in the universe full of knowledge available. Yet many puff up their egos and boast about their knowledge. Yet in their boasting they do not realize that they have stopped growing. Others will outgrow them and they will be left by themselves.

There are many ways to get lost by this trap. If we take a couple of these, it will be seen plainly. Just how many people who go to a martial arts class obtain a black belt and then stop going to class. You can ask them and they might say things like, "I've learned enough." "I've proven what I needed to prove." "I already reached the top." People look at a black belt as the pinnacle rank for martial arts. So many after reaching it will quit as they believe they have nothing left to learn. In actual earnesty, this is not the case. Actually it is a beginner's rank. It is especially emphasized in the curriculum I was a part of. The sashes you earn before black are essentially representing working up and building a foundation. Advanced martial concepts must be built off of a solid foundation. The black sash represents that your foundation is laid and now you can be taught for real. This is the real beginning of training.

Teaching is another trap. Becoming a teacher is another possible stumbling stone as many who start teaching get the impression that because they are the one in the room with knowledge, that then they are an important person. They become the one who dispenses the knowledge instead of the hungry student. The truth is that the best teachers are the ones who remain hungry students. Perhaps we teach now. Perhaps our teacher is gone. This does not mean we stop learning. There are learning opportunities all around us. We can learn from nature, life's happenings, our students. One of the best things that happened to me is that I started teaching. In teaching I have gone over so many of the concepts that I learned before now seeing them in a whole new light. And with student questions, there are so many things you might never have thought to ask about. No matter who we are, we should never stop being a hungry student.

Another trap is making accomplishments in tournaments and such things. Tournaments are good things. They give us a chance to practice with other practitioners, reach out and form a community. It is also good to test what we know as well as practice confidence in an unsure situation that may make one nervous. However the opportunities to fall into ego traps are just as great in number as the benefits. This is especially so in tournaments where the accolades are greater. Like world tournaments. The greater the accolades, the greater the potential trap. If someone would win in an international tournament, a possible conclusion that person might draw is that they are the best in the world. Not only is this foolish, but likely untrue. A more accurate conclusion would be that in that moment you were the best of those who signed up in that tournament. But even this isn't fully accurate. You don't fight everyone in a tournament. You fight winners in the bracket. Which means there are some you never fight. It is never clear enough to say that if you are beaten by someone, that the someone who beats them would also beat you. Perhaps they had a bad match. Or perhaps their skills were not optimized to fight that opponent, but they might do better against someone else.

Whatever the case, we have a champion. If being a black belt or a teacher wouldn't be enough, considering oneself a "champion" is an ego trap in itself. One such champion might have a disagreement with another practitioner. Such champions might use their accolade as validation for their argument. But it is important to remember that there is always a bigger fish. I cannot begin to tell you just how many "world champions" I've come across. By definition, there should only ever be one world champion, yet there are so many who can call themselves by that accolade. But it is also important to remember, these world champions are the champions of those who signed up in the tournament. Speaking honestly, the best practitioners I've come across don't spend their time attending tournaments.

Ultimately we must understand that no matter how far we go, there is still further to go. No matter how much we learn, there is still more to learn. No matter how good we get, there is always someone better. So there is no time to boast. We must move forward. And we must look at those around us as peers. No matter where anyone is in their journey, there is something to learn from them. We can ask those around us for help, and we can help those that are struggling, but ultimately we must move forward. We will never reach the end. There is no end to achieve. Only further growth. When we stop moving, then everything passes us by and we become trapped in our own self contained world. Be careful not to be stopped by your "self."

The Inadequate will try to Break Down the Adequate

Any time people try to do anything, there will always be naysayers. Now in the age of the internet there are more than ever before. The internet has connected humanity together. A person in Canada can talk to someone in India in seconds. Never before has humanity been able to communicate with each other so freely. But now that our circle has expanded, so has the amount of naysayers. It's simple math. The more people in a room, the greater the likelihood of having negative people in the bunch. As such the internet has given rise to negativity in this way.

It doesn't even matter the skill level of the practitioner. It could be a highly skilled practitioner, or it could be someone just beginning their journey. People will criticize them. They even do it under the guise of "constructive criticism" to try and appear as a good person or someone who knows. It really mucks up the waters for those who genuinely give constructive criticism in order to help the practitioner. But these naysayers use constructive criticism as a guise to say nasty things and get away with it. It's really just another form of bullying.

What many don't realize is that there are reasons that a person may act this way. These are more sad and broken human beings. Because why would anyone go out of their way to hurt another. If we try to understand why there are bullies and those that hurt, we can see that many had poor upbringings or have been hurt. If you try to pet a wild dog with a broken leg, you won't get its love, but its teeth. They are afraid and hurt. They see others reaching out as attempts to hurt them and will lash out in retaliation. Such a place is a place of great weakness. And we see when in a great place of weakness, out of fear the response is to act tough and scare off any possible attempts to harm you. It is less of a thoughtful attempt but an instant reaction.

Humans respond in the same way. Humans may have a more complicated psychology, but at the essence it is no different from a dog. If one considers the bully, perhaps their past has given them some great trauma creating these horrible responsive outbursts. Perhaps they were physically or mentally abused. This could give them many issues like a lack of self esteem. When one lacks self esteem, the natural instinctive response is to act tough in front of others to create a false front to ward off predators. In this case it may come in the form of verbal harassment berating someone's practice in an attempt to hide their own shortcomings. Perhaps why they insult is because they see themselves in the other person and verbally abuse them in an attempt to cover for their own lack in their practice. Mentally putting themselves above the one they abuse as it gives them comfort in the false idea of, "at least I'm better than that guy."

But this kind of response serves no one. It doesn't do anything for the one getting insulted. It only serves to create a false reality where we put ourselves above others, but in fact it has done none of that. We have proven nothing. We don't even know the other guy, and yet place ourselves above him in a reality of our own making. But this doesn't serve us. It only gives us a false comfort and halts our progress. By putting ourselves above others, we shut ourselves off to the opportunities to learn from them. Not only that, but the time used to berate them would be better used practicing.

Instead of living in a false reality by dragging others down, let us improve ourselves in the present moment. And remember to have compassion on those who hurt others, as they themselves are hurting. Remember that they are creating their own obstacles in their journey and creating their own pain. Do not criticize them back, but have pity. Criticizing them back will only cause them to clam up further and bark even louder. They are afraid whether they realize it or not. Have compassion, and keep training.

<u>The Fool Argues that a Hammer is Superior to the Screwdriver</u>

It is this very topic actually that my very first article was about. Many martial artists as well as outsiders looking in seem to think that certain styles are better than others. And those held in high regard vary depending on the individual giving their opinion. The thing is that this debate is actually rather silly and pointless when one comes to truly understand martial arts. First it is important to say that there are systems that are ineffective, but this has to do less with martial arts in general and more to do with the creation of said ineffective arts. Martial arts were created not as a sport, but a necessity. Back in the day, good martial skill could be the difference between making it home or dying on the way to get groceries. Styles made during such time were created from the experiences of those who were tried and tested regularly. However styles created nowadays don't have that experience to test their credibility. Certainly a better thing for society, but it leaves room for people with no martial experience to create systems. Systems created without experience are like a house built on sand.

In other cases, there are many intentional frauds that create systems as well. Karate used to be the new popular thing on the streets, and being the new, popular thing it created opportunities in the eyes of con-artists. They would create systems and build empires to take advantage of the attention to Karate. Unfortunately beginners with no martial experience don't know exactly what to look for, so scams like this are still effective today. When Bruce Lee became popular the attention shifted to Kung fu. New con-artists would create fake kung fu systems and old con-artists would change the name of their art to kung fu in order to take advantage of the shift. So there are indeed faulty systems, but it is mostly due to con-artists and incompetence.

But when talking of real time tested systems, the answer does not lie with the art being faulty, but the practitioner themselves. But many still argue. Modern martial arts vs traditional martial arts. Internal martial arts vs external martial arts. Northern vs southern. Eastern vs western. The list continues. Endless opportunities to create divide. It seems like a simple answer to those in the know, yet it remains an argument because of the many who don't know. They don't realize that they all have more in common than they do things that are different.

Not just in this debate, but in life people like to focus on the few things that are different than the many things they have in common. Internal and external stylists like to argue. Many internal stylists like to claim superiority for having internal skills. Modern artists like to claim superiority as they are the ones in the ring. Southern and northern Chinese martial artists like to disagree on the usage of hands and feet in contrast to each other.

This is all foolish debate. In my travels I have met internal martial artists with no internal skills and external martial artists with phenomenal internal skills. I have met good and bad martial artists of both the modern and traditional arts. I have met southern Chinese artists usually known for hand skills that have excellent foot skills and vice versa with northern. Low level martial artists will continue to waste their time debating like this while the high level artists will use that time to train and grow. The high level internal artist will look to the high level external artists and ask their opinion. The high level traditional artists will exchange notes between themselves and the high level modern martial artists. Those that know will not waste time claiming their style's superiority and instead use that time to learn and grow.

What many beginner martial artists don't realize is that the art they practice is not the end goal. Do not seek to be great Kung fu artists, jiu jitsu artists, etc. Styles and systems are not the skills, but the skills are obtained from the styles. Martial journeys are a mountain and all artists regardless of style are climbing the same mountain. Two styles may appear complete opposites, but it is just in appearance as perhaps they both started on opposite sides of the mountain and they can't see each other. But when climbing a mountain, you don't climb straight up. It is steep and it will tire you. Instead you zig zag. In time your path will cross with another path and you will meet someone of another system. But this intersection point means there are crossovers and similarities in the path and thus the style as well. The closer you get to the top, the more the mountain thins out and the more of these paths will cross. This means the further you go along your journey, the more you will see the similarities and the closer these arts appear to be. When you reach the peak you will see all the other artists of different styles there as well. Taking different paths to the same destination. The styles are not the mountain. The mountain is the art we all share. The styles are perspectives of the mountain. They are all correct in that they tell the story of the mountain, but not complete as they miss things about the mountain. Artists of other systems are our opportunities to see another perspective of the thing with practice.

The styles are the finger that is pointing at the moon. Don't get caught up staring at the finger. Look instead to the moon it is trying to direct you toward. If you get caught up in this silly debate, it means you got lost at the bottom of the mountain. Do not stagnate there in the misplaced bitter resentment. Work together with others to reach the peak. Styles cannot fight for themselves, it is the practitioner that makes the art. Don't get caught in traps. Just because there is a bad example of an art doesn't mean the art is bad. It is a pointless argument that has no bottom. It is a trap for the ego. Keep moving forward.

Tribalism

    Tribalism is defined as, "the state or fact of being organized in a tribe or tribes," or "the behavior and attitudes that stem from strong loyalty to one's own tribe or social group." This is actually a very common phenomenon that many people don't even realize they participate in. In the most simple of senses, it is being close to one's family, friends, and social circle. It is the way people try to survive in a less than ideal world. Maybe the world is on fire, but at least we have our family behind us. People may belittle us, but at least we have friends backing us up. This is indeed a good thing. Humans are social creatures and require bonds of some kind. And family helps us to keep on a good path. But of course with anything else, too much of a good something is a bad something.

    It is good to be loyal, but loyalty in toxic amounts creates a toxic mindset. When you call something good, this creates the concept of bad to contrast. If there are good people, then there must be bad people. This is the danger of creating scales. To acknowledge Yang creates Yin. Even if we only thought of calling our friends good, in our minds we have created the opposite. This creates an "us vs the world mentality. An "us vs them." In reality this is one of the most foolish things that we as humans continue to practice today. It shows in politics, religion, etc. You can't go on the internet without being bombarded with people trying to tear you down. This stems from tribalism.

We have borders to countries, differing political allegiances, so many things that cause divide instilled into culture. We all have yet to realize this folly. People from different countries are no different than us at the end of the day, yet we hear people mocking other countries while boasting of their own. They do not realize that they are the same. No matter what culture or upbringing, we are all just trying to make it through our lives. We all get hungry, we all suffer from trauma, we all want to find a circle to call home surrounded by people that love us.

Martial artists are no different. People argue over little insignificant things like the style they study vs another's. Whose teacher is better. Whose opinion is correct. But the more we lean into this mentality, the bigger the divide and the smaller the world of loved ones gets. At the end of the day, our personalities may differ, we may have different opinions, but at the heart of the matter there is no real difference between us and them.

Humanity together is strong. Divided we cannot stand. The state of the world is divided, so we create social circles to cope and help us through the troubling times. But imagine. If such a small social circle can help us, imagine the state of the world if every human worked together. Imagine the leaps and bounds in progress we could make. Imagine how much could be fixed. But so long as humans keep the tribalism mentality, this will never come to pass. But every change starts small. We must first start within ourselves. We must not contribute to the divide. We must look at everyone with compassion. Do not treat one person differently than anyone else. Do not treat them differently for status, political leaning, religion, race, gender, etc. Remember that those who can't get past this mentality are not evil people, just lost and confused. Have compassion as we were all there once. They are no different from us. When we see ourselves in them, then true understanding can happen. To quote something I read the other day, "Opinion is the lowest form of human knowledge. It requires no accountability, no understanding. The highest form of knowledge is Empathy, for it requires us to suspend our egos and live in another's world." (Bill Bullard). To look at others with empathy, this is the way to understanding. This is the way to understanding that the people that we once hated are no different than us. We are all lost and confused trying to make it through our lives. So have compassion on those who are lost, and that compassion will come back to you. That is what Karma is.

<u>To Lose is to Win, Boasting Comes Alongside Insecurity</u>

In life there is a stigma that success and winning is something to strive for and that one should avoid failure and losing. For martial artists this may manifest itself in different ways such as winning or losing a tournament, defeating our opponent in sparring, successfully completing a training regimen, etc. But such an outlook is damaging. It gives an unrealistic look at life that breeds deep insecurities in one's mind.

The very concept of winning implies that there is losing, and the concept of success creates the concept of failure. But one does not exist without the other. There is a relationship between the two concepts, not a duality. No person is successful and no person is a failure. A person may appear to be successful with monetary gain, but that person may have failures in other aspects of their life, not to mention that their visible success was built upon a mountain of failures.

Success does not breed success, but failure. Failure does not breed failure, but success. For through failure we learn where our flaws are, and in knowing this we know where and how we can improve. Thus failure brings us success. To take sparring as an example, one will learn far more through losing than they would through winning. The loss that happens in a sparring match would represent a moment of one's death. But it is not a literal death, it is a figurative one. We will have chances after this to try again rather than it ending. But with this loss, we are now armed with the knowledge of how we were defeated. This knowledge and experience will then allow us to meet similar circumstances and recognize that the way we lost before was not the way we should take, thus we try another. We may do this and theoretically "die" again. That teaches us another way not to do things. We continue again and again, failing again and again until one time we succeed. This moment teaches us the way to move forward through such an obstacle. We will then always be armed with the experience and knowledge of how to proceed to such a situation.

      Through losing, we learned to win. But this has its own danger, as through winning, we learn to lose. With enough success, we develop ourselves in it. We learn that we are successful and that we know what we are doing. This breeds the danger of the braggart. The danger of the one who is full of themself. With such an attitude they forget the losses that their success was built on. With success on the brain everything else becomes a loss in their mind. Other's successes become failures before their own successes. They then shut themselves away, believing they are the ones that know. Passing by many opportunities to learn from others who have experienced more. They become the big fish in a small pond and never grow to their potential. But if they can avoid their own ego trap and continue the cycle of failure and success, nothing will stop them.

Thus we shouldn't fear failure, nor overextend ourselves for the sake of success. Rather we should be the passive observer appreciating the cycle as it comes as we continue through our daily lives. Not striving, yet leaving nothing undone. Too much celebration of success breeds egotism, too much fear of failure breeds depression. Rather Enjoy the fruits of success as if walking and enjoying the smell of flowers. Enjoying them while they are there, but not missing them when they are gone. Enjoy the trials of failure, for through enduring them we become reborn. To try to have one without the other is to have neither of them. Success and failure are two aspects of the same thing. Do not rush to success, or you will stumble over failure. Do not try to ignore the failure that is coming, or you will never see success. Instead observe and enjoy.

Shedding the Ego

Do the opposite

Among my martial family, we have a certain rule that we learned from George Xu (Xu Guoming) that we then dubbed, "The rule of Xu." This rule is, "Everybody sucks, so look at what they do and do the opposite." One may look at it as crude, but the more one advances the more it rings true. There are a lot more bad examples out there than good ones. In the workforce it is described as 80% of anybody in any profession is average to below average. 20% of people are actually good at what they do. Martial Arts being a niche field with a steep learning curve makes it more like 90/10. While 1% could be dubbed as titans/legends.

It is a good goal to look toward this top percent finding great masters to learn from or be inspired by, but if that is all we look toward then we lose 90% of our opportunities to learn. Taking the rule of Xu into account, we can literally learn from anybody. We can learn from one practitioner noticing they talk a lot of hype for themselves, but in that time they are flapping their gums, they could be training. So it's an opportunity to learn. Less time talking, more time practicing. Another practitioner may be tense when practicing. So we must instead relax so that our body's movement is unobstructed.

To only learn from good examples only lets us grow 10% of the time. So once we have gained enough perspective, we can look at these bad examples and learn just as much as we could through the good examples. There comes a time in training down the road where these examples must become far more abstract. One day without fail, our teachers will move on or pass away. Our good examples will leave and we will be left with the need to find examples again. It is then we must understand that our examples are not limited to people. One can watch the water moving in a creek. They see debris catching on a rock while the water continues to flow around unobstructed. They can say, "I shouldn't be like the debris getting caught up by the obstructions, rather I should be like the water flowing freely without impediment.

No matter where we are in our journey, there is no lack of lessons to be learned, so long as one opens themselves to them. So always look around and keep your eyes open. Watch people practice and analyze. One may have bad knee alignment that has caused them knee pains, so look at what they do and do the opposite. One practitioner may have gone too soft in their approach. They are inspired by softness and now they can't fight their way out of a wet paper bag. So look at what they do and do the opposite. One may be too stiff and tense, look at what they do and do the opposite. One may fixate their mind on a singular objective like taking someone to the ground or only striking the head, causing them to miss many openings and opportunities because they were too tunnel visioned in their approach. Look at what they do and do the opposite. Whenever you feel plateaued in your progress, do the opposite. Experiment, try something different, never stagnate.

Truth Appears Differently to Different People, But Still Remains as Truth

One can say, "we don't practice high kicks, only kicks to the waist and lower." Another will practice high kicks. One will say they emphasize striking, while another emphasizes grappling. One will fight at short range, the other long range. One will say strike as if you were a knife penetrating flesh, another will say to strike like you were swinging a lead pipe. One will say be direct, the other will say be circular. To say any one of these are incorrect would be but the result of a limited worldview. With seemingly opposing viewpoints, one might naturally come to the conclusion that one must be correct and the other wrong. But in actuality they are all simultaneously correct. If we limit ourselves to a linear way of thinking, then we won't see that these thoughts that seem counter to each other are actually two sides of the same coin.

We see proof of all of these previous claims. We've seen plenty of knockouts from kicks to the face, yet we've also seen people attempt high kicks and get swept. Both of these ideas have merit. What we learn is that high kicks are effective, but they also leave large openings. A high risk, high reward concept. We see grapplers takedown and submit strikers, and we see strikers knockout grapplers. So what about this can we learn overall? Really that multiple seemingly opposing opinions can all be correct simultaneously.

These are all perspectives about martial arts. But perspectives are not everything. Perspectives actually dilute truth. To have any viewpoint creates bias. These biases eventually become so deeply embedded into ourselves that we don't even realize we have biases. These biases influence how we see things, so we never see the full truth. But then there leaves the question of how one sees the truth. If we never look from outside our own perspective, then the truth will elude us forever. The answer lies in other perspectives.

If we can't see the truth, we ask another for truth. In asking, we attempt to understand them and their viewpoint. With enough time we can understand and see the world from their perspective too. Then we have two ways to see the world. From this we can see the overlap and similarities. We can also see contrast. We continue to look and ask, attempting to obtain multiple perspectives. But again these perspectives are not the truth, but they point us toward the truth. It is important to not mistake the finger pointing at the moon for the moon itself.

With enough time we have many perspectives to look through, but our work is not done. It is then that we must overlap the perspectives, compare and contrast. Chip away at the extraneous. Over time one can see more that these perspectives share and that they share more than the differences that they have. These things they share again point us at the truth.

With enough time and training, we can remove the perspectives entirely. The extraneous is gone, and we are left with the truth. Styles are like this.

Styles are different perspectives on the truth of martial arts. Each style can give their perspective on what martial arts should be based on their views. Not one of them is the full truth, but they all point towards truth. Eventually we must let go of our own perspective in order to see the image of truth clearly. In doing so we gain the perspective of non-perspective. The perspective that has no influence and is completely unbiased. When one achieves this perspective, then no knowledge is out of their reach. So long as the work is done, they will find the truth, because they realize that truth is not limited to one point, but there are infinite facets of truth. They will not be limited by their own minds and will grow.

Knowing that We Don't Know

Contrary to what some may think, humility is actually a good sign of intelligence. Someone who is quick to tell you that they don't know is more likely to have greater knowledge and wisdom. In the pursuit of knowledge, it can be likened to that of someone walking on a trail. In the beginning of said trail, the thicket is so great that it is hard to see through, making it hard to see that far ahead of you. This is what it is like for a beginner. They can't see that far ahead of themselves. A person with a mind of someone who hasn't walked very far down this trail will start to make assumptions about that which they cannot see. This is an attempt to "fill in the blanks" in their knowledge of the things they can't see. They do this because their subconscious realizes there is something missing and will create something to fill the space. But being a beginner without knowledge of the thing they are studying, that filler will likely not be accurate information. This creates a sense of ego as the person reflects their limited knowledge on that which they don't know. When someone reflects their ego in this way, the info they reflect upon becomes very personal as it is the reflection of their own knowledge. Thus they become furious when their opinions are questioned. At such times we must refer to the phrase, "Empty carts make noise."

However the further one walks the path, the more clear things become. The less thicket there is, and the more one can see ahead of them. When spending enough time on a subject learning its foundations, one can start to see that which they couldn't before, and while they may not know some things, at this point they can come to understand that which they don't know. One can be told a concept in martial arts and it might make sense to them, but putting it into practice might prove difficult. This is such an example of something that they know that they don't know. The more we practice, the more things we don't know reveal themselves to us. Once revealed, we can practice them in an attempt to know them eventually. But until that time they are something that we can see yet admit that we don't know.

The more we continue, the more things we see but admit that we don't know. But to the uneducated, they don't know much and assume to know things, but it is false knowledge. There is much that they don't know that they don't know. But after we walk the path for some time, we get the benefit of retrospective. This retrospective allows us to see and remember the things we've gone through on our journey. We can look back on all the things that at one point we didn't know that we didn't know about. Now those things could be things that we know or things that we know we don't know about. And looking at all these things that we didn't know that we didn't know before, we can infer that there are things that we currently don't know that we don't know about.

With the current mind of knowing that there are things that we don't know that we don't know, it gives the motivation for a hungry student to push forward. To learn things that we don't know we don't know. But this also gives us something else. For in accepting that we don't know things and understanding there is so much to learn, we gain humility. We accept that these journeys for knowledge never end, and the more we know, the more is revealed that we don't know. The ego gets tinier and tinier as the knowledge we don't know becomes an infinitely expanding cosmos. We become a tiny spec in this cosmos and we see the beauty of understanding that no matter how far we go, we will never even come close to this large expanse of information. One may look at the cosmos and decide not to try and give up completely, but these people did not go far, as this is just a hurdle along the pursued path, but the hungry student will look at it as beauty. Seeing something far greater than themselves and just being happy to play their part. This is where knowledge creates humility and then one starts to gain wisdom.

That being said, it still is not so black and white. There will be times along the passage where we see all sorts of things that we know we don't know and are able to work on said things. Yet there are times where these things may come to an end and we are left with what we know and the things we don't know we don't know. This is where many of the ego traps come in. People who think they've "made it" by becoming a teacher, black belt, won tournaments, etc. These ego traps are a test by life to see if you've truly let go of your ego. It weens out the foolish from the earnest.

The earnest student, instead of thinking that they know all will instead say, "There must be something I don't know. I must find it!" This is the point where one must change where they are looking. For some this may mean looking for a new teacher. It may be seen as disrespectful by some, but an earnest teacher will always want their student to succeed above their own ego. If one teacher could only get them so far, one must pay proper respects and thank them for their time, but one must go find a teacher that can help them further down the road. A good student will learn from the teacher and attempt to take it further. A good teacher will help raise the student and simultaneously take their own journey further. We must not be trapped by the ego, but instead realize the infinite cosmos of knowledge never ends and gaze upon the beauty that humanity will never fully grasp.

Lu Dong Bin's Invisible sword

Lu Dong Bin (leader of the 8 immortals of Daoist legend) has many stories surrounding him. There is record of him being a real person, but like any legend it is followed by embellishment. That being said, there are many things to learn from his life and legend. The first of which is his depiction of carrying his sword in a sheath on his back. Anyone who studies the history of swordsmanship in any culture knows that the old depiction of carrying the sword on one's back is largely a movie trope. This is because having a sword sheathed on one's back makes drawing the sword a huge inconvenience. This makes it dangerous for the swordsman who needs to draw his blade quickly for defense. The more common way to carry one's sword is in a sheath on one's hip. Particularly on the opposite hip to the swordsman's dominant arm so that one can easily draw it with their sword hand.

So while it may seem to be a mistake on Lu's part, rather I think it speaks to his character. Lu was known for his sword skills. He wasn't a simple fool. Having the sword on his back suggests he never intends to use it while still having it in case it is needed. To be such a well known swordsman while never intending to use it seems like a contradiction. But to knowingly have power over other's lives and choosing not to use and abuse that power shows good character. Lu Dong Bin has become a symbol of restraint. Having power, yet choosing not to use it.

This is the truth of inner strength. To have the power in one's reach to do whatever you want and choose instead to not use it for one's own gain. That is what this teaches.

Another story that goes along with this is one where a warlord had kidnapped He Xian Gu (the depicted female of the 8 immortals). Lu Dong Bin went out to free her. When he arrived, he was greeted by the warlord and his army. He demanded that they free He Xian Gu and the warlord refused. Upon this response Lu draws and raises his sword. Upon seeing this happen, the entire army surrenders because they knew of Lu's legendary sword skills. This story teaches us the "when" and "how" of using power. He does not arrive with a drawn sword in hand, but it is still on his back when he faces the army. This means that power and violence should never be used first, but instead as a last resort for the greater good. When he arrives, first he demands her freedom. Diplomacy before violence. Upon their refusal, it is only then that he draws his sword. Only when it is the last option is when he draws his sword. Upon seeing this, the army surrenders. Lu knew others considered his swordsmanship to be superior, but he knew the tolls of violence. So he resorts to it last. But upon resorting to violence, his reputation does the slaughtering for him. Winning the battle of the minds before the battle of fists could happen. Demoralization is another path to victory without violence. In the end, he reminded them of his power, but never had to use it.

One last story is a legend surrounding his sword. This legend depicts his sword as magical in that when drawn it would be invisible to the eye. The opponent's would never see their deaths coming and it would be over in an instant. This shows us that when using our power, how it should be used. No extraneous flashes, no drawing it out longer than necessary, no shows of power. Once relied upon, using it for the task and then putting it away. When one has a seat of power, a weak minded fool will flaunt it to hide their insecurities. They will try to draw attention to their greatness like a middle school bully. Instead use it for what needs to be done, then put it away. No longer drawing attention to oneself. One should not delight in violence, greed, and use of power. One should truly delight in never needing to resort to barbaric needs.

As martial artists in today's world, we do not hold as much power as in the days preceding guns, but that does not mean we don't hold any power. There are still moments where we could hold life and death in our hands. What these stories teach us is how to use it responsibly. Whether using it to protect someone from an attacker or to help an elder cross the street. Both cases one should get the job done and not look for praise and not show off. Just complete the task and be on your way. We all hold responsibility in our actions and the things we are involved in. Let us not use our ability for self-gain.

Acid Hurts the Container it is Held In

Anger is like acid. Our body is a container. Our body will contain whatever we put in it. When we harbor anger within ourselves, it is like pouring acid into our container. Over time acid damages the container it is held in as that is what acid does. Anger in our body does the same. It wears us down and drains us. The longer we hold on, the more it hurts us. Stress has been proven to affect the body negatively with effects that resemble aging. Thus the importance of letting go of anger is paramount.

The world is filled with moments that will test our patience to its limits. Whether it be people trying our patience or things going wrong, the choice is the same. We can hold onto it, or let it go. The concept of letting go appears simple, yet it is incredibly difficult. Anger is like a fire. Things that create fire have addictive properties. In Chinese medicine as well as martial arts, fire is used to describe the nature of certain ailments and practices. There are several practices in martial arts that I have been taught that are fire practices, and I have been forewarned about their danger from those that have experienced it firsthand. Fire is very useful in many things. We can look at it in very literal uses like early versions of a train using fire to power the engine. Progress through fire methods also are typically quicker. But these practices are dangerous as this faster way of progress can become addictive and lead the practitioner to get burned.

Much like alcohol and other addictive substances, they give us happy immediate benefits, but affect our health overtime. We know that the liver must work to break down the alcohol we consume and in Chinese medicine it is again compared to setting the liver on fire. Over time this taxation on the liver will take its toll. Our ability to drink and be fine the next day worsens and so do the hangovers. Yet we continue to be drawn to the addictive properties.

The fire practices are like this. The benefits are great and we continue. But overtime these benefits will seemingly lessen. This is because the body is getting used to the practice, so the feeling one gets afterward will continue to lessen. Yet many people make the mistake of seeing this as a problem and not as a progression. They see it as that they are not gaining the benefits from before. So they will chase those benefits by practicing more intensely. The problem is that the fire had never died down, we just got used to it. So in practicing more intensely they are creating a bigger fire that will lead them down the path of cinders and sickness. One in an example of drug usage may find that the light drugs they are using don't give them the benefits it used to and they may branch out to try more dangerous things to stoke the flames.

This condition is called "fire chasing demons" in Chinese medicine. Chasing fire will deteriorate the body and mind leading to craziness as well as physically manifested ailments like redness of skin and rising body heat. This is the danger of chasing fire. It is much the same as holding in anger. Allowing oneself to take out their anger on the matter that angers them can feel good in the moment, but over time its problems will make themselves apparent. That person that cut us off in traffic, that guy that said something rude to us, our morning coffee that spilled on the floor, they are all done. It is in the past. The longer we let such things bother us, the longer it will harm us. With such a weakened container, how could we be in the shape we need to practice martial arts. The body erodes and is weakened. The mind erodes and we get tunnel vision. It is important to let these things go, so that the past will not destroy our present and future.

My teacher told me the importance of balancing any fire practice with a water practice. Anything addictive that causes rising must be balanced with something calming, relaxing, settling. Any anger must be met with patience, forgiveness, and understanding. Never light a fire without a way to put it out. Fire will look for ways to feed itself and grow. With its growth it will cause more damage. Let go, release, and be free.

If You "Can't" Do It, Then You are Right

      People are generally familiar with phrases like, "Mind over matter." What this quote basically means is that the mind controls our bodies. Truly the mind and body are not two different things as both are interconnected and affect each other to an intimate degree. Like when one catches sickness after fretting over it for some time, or when one heats up the body simply by believing they are heating up. The mind affects the body, but also the body affects the mind.

      When one slumps their shoulders, looks downwards, and concaves their chest, very reminiscent of someone who is depressed, they are more likely to be tired, sad, or depressed. Much to the same degree, someone who extends the chest slightly and looks forward is more likely to be content. Again, the mind and body are not two separate things, but instead are an integrated whole. The body affects the mind and the mind affects the body.

      So from this we can say with confidence that if we believe something with our mind, then we will embody that thing. Through training, martial artists use this concept to apply to things like a tiger mindset. To embody the spirit and mindset of a tiger. Something that hunts and feeds, not fights. This is an attempt to remove the emotional factor of a fight as emotional response inhibits proper martial response. So in many cases like this, this concept is used for training. However, it is as much if not more dangerous as it is helpful.

One must not be afraid to use this concept, but also they should tread carefully. Whatever you put in your mind regularly, you will become. If you regularly put negative things into your mind, negative results will come out. One such example is the word "can't." People use this word often. And in many of those cases they wrongly use the word in place of "won't," or even use it to express their non-belief in themselves. In the case of those who don't believe in themselves, they will prove themselves right the more they choose to express that they "can't." Feeding that thought to ourselves overtime will only demotivate ourselves further inhibiting ourselves.

One other such way some use can't I have noticed is when referring to a comparison between oneself and one's teacher. There are many boons to having a good or famous teacher, but there also comes drawbacks. One such drawback is the very comparison of teacher to student. Especially when one puts their teacher on a pedestal, they figuratively put their teacher beyond their reach. They start to think, "I could never be as good as my teacher." Some even become complacent with the feeling and shrug it off. However this thinking is exactly the reason they will never reach their teacher. They inhibit themselves mentally before they ever could have gotten there. Even the very comparison of teacher to student is fundamentally wrong. One's teacher is their teacher.

There can never be another teacher like them as everyone is their own person. So one should not try to be their teacher, but instead try to be the best version of themselves. In being the best version of themselves, they will never be their teacher, but they might very well surpass their teacher in skill. So long as they approach things the right way.

The mind is a powerful and dangerous thing. It is why meditation training becomes so important. To empower, focus and to have control over one's own mind. This allows us to take ourselves far. But without that discipline, our mind will be the very thing that holds us back. If you believe you "can't" do it, then you are right.

Daoist Thought

The Dao that Can be Told

(Old Taiji Symbol)

The 1st chapter of the Dao De Jing in one translation reads as follows:

"The Dao that can be told is not the eternal (true) Dao. The name that can be named is not the eternal name. The nameless is the beginning of heaven and earth. The named is the mother of ten thousand things. Ever desireless, one can see the mystery. Ever desiring, one can see its manifestations. These two spring from the same source, but differ in name. This appears as darkness. Darkness within darkness. The gate to all mystery."

So the Dao (way) that can be told is not the true Dao. You guessed it. If I or another were to tell you about the way, it wouldn't be the true way. The path that we teach to you is not the true path. There is no such true path that someone can show to you. For that path would not be the path. But what does this mean to us? It means that the way can not be given or shown. It can only be found or experienced. No matter how hard we try, every one of us on earth is biased. This bias comes from our life's experiences. It is said that to a cheater, everyone cheats. To a thief, everyone steals. For those people, the color of their world has changed to match their actions. To a thief who steals daily, stealing becomes normal. Just another fact of life. So it is easy for the thief to say, "everyone steals." To another it may be an unspeakable offense. But this shows bias.

Bias affects our views and how we interact. These things can be as obvious as the two examples I've mentioned, or so subtle that one might barely notice. But everyone has them. Thus when trying to communicate with others, these biases can easily influence how we communicate or receive information in an exchange. Someone can say that they accidentally misplaced one of your belongings and we might react and think they stole it even if they were telling us the truth. The colors of our mind change what we see.

So the true Dao cannot be told. It cannot be named. For if it was, it wouldn't be the true Dao. The person attempting to tell us about the Dao and give us its name, as earnest as they might be in attempting to do so, cannot give us the true Dao. For they, no matter the great or little amount, have biases of their own. This bias is a filter for the information to go through before it reaches you. They will speak from their own experiences and those experiences will alter the truth. The experiences are not the truth, but they are the person's exposure to the truth. The truth is the same for all, but the experiences all differ. Yet the experiences are our visceral understanding of the Dao and thus we speak about the Dao with our experiences. So as we speak it, we already unknowingly alter the Dao that we speak about. Coming to understand this is part of the journey to understanding the Dao.

After the altered Dao is spoken, the recipient then must receive it. However the recipient's bias also alters the Dao. For as the recipient receives the information, it goes through their own bias filter as they attempt to understand it. It is understood by comparing and contrasting their experiences thus far. By the time it is received fully, it has been altered twice. This is to be understood and accepted. It is human. The more we grow and experience, the more our views and understandings change as well. Our understanding of the Dao we were told will change accordingly.

The Dao will not come to us in a moment. It is an entire life of chipping away the stone until the statue (the dao) can truly be revealed. It is a process that leads to realizations. Not a one time sudden change.

However all this said, it should be understood that while no one can hand us the Dao, it doesn't mean we should shut potential teachers out. While they cannot tell us the way, they can help us in the right direction. There is a saying about the teacher pointing at the moon. Let us not get caught up in the finger that points. That is the biased filter. But instead look toward the moon (the Dao). The teacher points the way, however from this we do not receive understanding. We must still walk down the path to understanding ourselves and experience the moon firsthand.

In our journey we may experience many conflicting interpretations of the Dao. We might think that one has to be right while the other is wrong. However to hold the paradoxes of conflicting truths both being correct simultaneously is part of the journey. One may say you can only find the Dao after endless meditation in a monastery where there are no distractions. Another may say they found it while farming one day. Still another may have found it on the field of battle. All these differ in name, but they sprung from the same source which is the Dao. All these paths are correct paths. While there do exist incorrect paths, one must understand there is not only one correct path, but many.

If someone says, "I know the way and no one else does," they are deluded or a liar. Martial arts is one path to the Dao, and there are many branching paths across the systems. No one art is the only path to the Dao. They are the differing experiences that point the way to the Dao. In the same way no single martial art will give you martial skill alone, but they are all paths to martial skill. They all may appear different and differ in name, but they all spring from the same source. They all start at different points, but they all eventually spiral inwards towards the center and reach the Dao. Once all the extraneous is chipped off, we are left only with the Dao. At that point we are not all masters of other arts, but we all are members of the Dao. Not a boxer, not a painter, not a cook, but we all find we were always children of the Dao.

One Can Know Beauty as Beauty Because There is Ugliness

The second chapter of the Dao De Jing reads:

"Under heaven all can know beauty as beauty only because there is ugliness. All can know good as good only because there is evil. Therefore having and not having arise together. Difficult and easy compliment each other. Long and short contrast each other. High and low rest upon each other. Voice and sound harmonize each other. Front and back follow one another. Therefore the wise go about doing nothing, teaching - no-talking. Ten thousand things rise and fall without cease. Creating, yet not possessing. Working, yet not taking credit. Work is done, then forgotten. Therefore it lasts forever."

For the next two chapters, let's split this passage in two. For this section, we will focus on, "Under heaven all can know beauty as beauty only because there is ugliness. All can know good as good only because there is evil. Therefore having and not having arise together. Difficult and easy compliment each other. Long and short contrast each other. High and low rest upon each other. Voice and sound harmonize each other. Front and back follow one another."

This passage directly speaks about the concept of Taiji. This concept of Taiji is the same concept that would later influence martial arts and even lead to the creation of the term Taijiquan which would be used to refer to a popular martial art. This "Taiji" would be referred to by many as Yin/Yang. Yin/Yang means dark/bright. Taiji in this context refers to the idea of Yin/Yang interchange. Many wrongly refer to it as Yin "and" Yang, but this is incorrect as it implies Yin/Yang to be binary which creates duality. But Yin/Yang is not duality and this passage suggests it too. This passage talks about these opposing concepts like beauty and ugliness as if they were the same thing, for they are just two sides of the same coin. Both concepts exist as they are not separate concepts, but two ends of the same spectrum. Acknowledging one end creates the other. For if we did not know about ugliness, we couldn't know what beauty is. We only know what beauty is because we have the concept of ugliness. It is from this spectrum that we can compare and contrast things and say one thing is ugly while the other is beautiful.

However, without the beautiful thing to contrast, the ugly thing no longer becomes ugly, but it is considered normal. Take movies for example. During the time when movies were a new concept and there wasn't much material to compare, there were many movies that people would say were good. But now looking back after decades of the industry, many of those films we could say we're pretty bad now that we have new stuff to compare. It was good for the time, but with the improved technology and improved acting skills as people learned more over their careers, we now have extended the spectrum and what was beautiful before might now appear ugly. Of course these things are subjective and nostalgia might influence, but we all acknowledge the phenomenon that things can age well or poorly as new things come out to compare with.

We can see from this that the spectrum is affected the more extremes are introduced. These opposites do not exist in a vacuum, otherwise the phenomenon we mentioned would not exist. Thus opposites like good and evil also exist on such a scale. However, first mentioning a scale can give the impression of a linear graph. It would actually be more accurate to have it represented as a circle. These opposites are not separate sides, but rather they feed into each other as the varying degrees of yin/yang flow into each other. There isn't Yin without Yang, but Yang exists inside Yin to varying degrees and vice versa. So good and evil as we experience in humanity are not separate, but together.

Yin exists in Yang, while Yang lives in Yin. We all know that a well intentioned person can do bad things. If the context of Yin=evil and Yang=good, then this would be Yang existing within Yin as outwardly bad things are done, but the inward intentions were good. There are also those who do good things for bad reasons. Donating and helping others for clout and recognition instead of simply doing the right thing. This then would be Yin within Yang. And no one is perfect. People constantly fluctuate in this interchange both on a small everyday scale like having good days and days where you are fed up, as well as on a larger scale where big life changes happen and we change the way we are as a person, like a high school bully who turns his life around. Nothing ever stays the same forever.

In martial arts if attack=Yang and defense=Yin, then we can look at fighting with this spectrum. Both attack and defense are important and without either, we will be missing something. With no defense, we are open like someone who was never taught to keep his hands up to guard their face. Without attack we are left without options to end the encounter and will lose when we tire from blocking so much. There must be both. Even if we take martial arts that like to be towards one end of the spectrum like Xingyiquan and Xinyiliuhe which prefer attack over defense, they are not void of defense. Arts like these have few blocks, but their attacks become their blocks. Using their attacks to deflect incoming attacks while on the way to their target. This is Yin within Yang.

To choose an extreme in any situation is to deny that extreme as well. Denying one is to deny both. Accepting one means to accept both. Not accepting this is to blind oneself to reality. We see so much conflict in the world because many view others and their ideas as different, but they spring from the same source. Humans are not that different from one another. Those that say others are bad and different fall victim to their human condition that we all share. We can all see we have imperfections. This is the first thing to acknowledge we all share. From this foundation we will see the ten thousand things as one thing as this circular spectrum makes itself known.

Eating Bitter

To elaborate further into the meaning of the first part of chapter two, I will give another possible context to the chapter. It is important to remember that these chapters are not locked into one particular meaning, but could have many meanings and interpretations depending on the context. That meaning to some might even change over time as the practitioner is exposed to new experiences. So the context I'd like to give now is appreciation for both sides of the coin.

For one to truly appreciate one concept, the other concept must be appreciated as well. For many in training, they might have heard the phrase, "Eating bitter to taste sweet." If we only ever eat sweet things, we will soon lack appreciation for sweet things. If one has never tasted sweet before, upon tasting sweetness they will experience the sweetness more than someone who regularly tastes sweet. The sweetness might even be overpowering to the one who hasn't regularly tasted sweet. Yet the properties of the sweet food have not changed. What was different was the two people. To the sweet taster, the sweet was so normal it became bland. To the other a whole new sensation was experienced.

The one who regularly tastes sweet cannot truly appreciate sweet, however upon tasting something bitter, they'll immediately have something to contrast and will then appreciate the sweet. This can be taken in many directions, but we'll focus on what it means to a martial artist. In martial arts there are many foundational exercises that are no fun to do for anyone. Horse stance is one of the classic examples. No one wants to sit in a horse stance with the thighs parallel to the ground for extended durations. Such a practice is bitter.

Contrasting, practicing forms and sparring might be seen as far more interesting. Getting to perform cool moves, applying them in combat. It's like eye candy. While both of these practices are essential in and of themselves alone they are empty. One must have a solid foundation to build skills off of form and sparring practice. One can practice just the latter two and still get decent martial arts, but those without foundation will crumble before those that suffer bitter. Just one such benefit from horse stance is stable stepping. You can do forms and sparring all day, but if you are easily swept off your feet, then an advanced practitioner will pick one apart.

For it is the tasting of bitter that allows us to taste sweet. Truly a better way to look at practice I find is that true sweet can't be found in the practices themselves. This is a sort of false sweet. The fools' gold of sweet. True sweet rather is a result of eating bitter. It is like that feeling after a good workout. That feeling when your body releases its stress and you feel lighter. That feeling that happens after immense suffering during the workout. That feeling when the workout is over and you have that moment to reflect on the work that is done. The appreciation that comes with it. The skills that will develop as a result. That is true sweetness. Now speaking of the work that is

done, it is time to move onto the next part of the
chapter.

Work is Done and Then Forgotten

For a refresher on the second part of the verse:

"Therefore the wise go about doing nothing, teaching - no-talking. Ten thousand things rise and fall without cease. Creating, yet not possessing. Working, yet not taking credit. Work is done, then forgotten. Therefore it lasts forever."

The meaning of this verse is profound, yet many miss this aspect in their own lives. This verse really reflects the idea of living in the moment. Not dwelling in the past nor worrying for the future. To truly do nothing, does not mean doing "nothing," but rather doing "no-thing." "Nothing" doesn't truly exist. Everything is actually something. Atoms exist in the air as gasses even though we can't see them. And if we were to lie in bed all day, people would refer to it as doing "nothing," yet we breathe, we think, we lie there, perhaps sleep. Even when sleeping our mind still processes events of the day. Everything has substance, yet also it has non-substance. For between the atoms, there is empty space. Substance and non-substance, but the non-substance is also its own substance. More will be elaborated on this in the section of the book focusing on Buddhist thought.

To live in the moment using the examples in the text, teaching, no-talking. Do not talk about your past achievements as if to brag. It provides us with nothing and only serves to inflate the ego. Instead use it to teach. The experiences of the past shouldn't trap our minds, but instead use them to learn and teach others in the present moment, then let them go. Don't use the moments of teaching to gloat about the teachings either. This is defeating the entire purpose. Create, yet don't possess. The things we create can in themselves become our prison. If we attach ourselves to our creations, it is no different than willingly putting oneself in a prison. Instead let go of your creations. They may help society, or may just be a pretty rock, however in the end we are done creating. We are now living in another present moment. Let the past go. Do not suffer yearning for the past. Working and not taking credit. The work we do in the moment at another point in time is done. No need to keep our mind on it. Reflecting after a job well done is healthy and it informs us in time to come. But the work is done, we must stop dwelling. Claiming credit in this context means essentially to hold onto one's accomplishments. Not necessarily that if someone asks us what we did that we have to lie, but not lord credit as a badge of honor. In time this might even reveal itself as more the type of person who will do a kindness and purposefully do so with no one around. To do work not for glory, but for it not to be undone.

Truly when one holds onto the work they do, the work is lost on them. They will be so caught up in past accomplishments that they will miss the work in the moment. But to do the work and forget it makes it last forever. The work was done. We are wiser for it. We move forward. Martial arts is no different. We get done with tough routines. We might even make breakthroughs in our practice. Dwelling on them though stops us on the road of our journey. Instead they must be let go. Then the rewards of the work arise, but not when one seeks them. Instead when not seeking them do they reveal themselves.

5 Colors Blind the Eyes

12th chapter of the Dao De Jing:

"The 5 colors blind the eye. The 5 tones deafen the ear. The 5 flavors dull the mouth. Racing through the field and hunting make the mind wild. Searching for precious goods leads astray. Therefore, the sage attends to the belly, and not to what he sees. He rejects the latter and chooses the former."

To simplify this chapter, it comes down to our perception of reality vs reality itself. People live their entire lives living in the world they perceive to be one way when in reality, it is not. The 5 colors, 5 tones, 5 tastes represent our experiences. The experiences that we gather along our lives changes the way we perceive things. For example, to someone who has been scammed out of their money, suddenly everyone in their sight has ulterior motives and is a potential crook.

When we experience something, we take it very personally. An experience is a visceral example of how reality can happen in one moment. The trap is that that experience doesn't reveal the whole truth of reality, but only a momentary truth. For a person born to a rich family, they may get everything they want upon request. This is their perceived reality that they experience and believe to be true. But when they go out on their own and now lack their parent's financial backing, they may request and not receive. This is their perceived reality crumbling. Many will refuse this reality and live in denial. Unfortunately many unknowingly live in denial like this their entire lives and never realize even upon death. They have lived with this perceived reality for so long that they can conceive no other reality than their own perceived one.

One's experiences color one's views of the world. If one wears glasses with red shaders and never removes them, the world will appear more red to them. At first one may understand that it is not reality, but with enough time they can conceive no other way, but the one they experience. The problem lies in that while aspects of their perceived reality may be true, for much of the rest they will conceive and believe lies based off of their bias. This leads to delusion, and rejection of other's perceptions of reality. This creates quarreling. No matter what one may think, not a human alive can say that they themselves have escaped this concept of their own perception of reality. Those who claim to be completely unbiased are usually the most biased. Removing bias is a lifelong process.

To come to understand and work on this process, one first must acknowledge that their views do not always equal reality. They may coincide on some truths, but we will ultimately miss the truth. We must look to others to learn how they perceive the world. Be careful not to only search like minded people, or you risk creating an echo chamber that will hide the truth from you forever. Find those whose views differ. Learn and understand their perceived reality. Do this with everyone you see. Eventually things will clear up. With enough views, truth will reveal itself more and more. You take and apply the shaders of others. You may have seen the world in red before, but now you can see it in blue, yellow, orange, etc. Understand that each of these views work towards the truth, but none of them are the truth itself. They simply give you another way to look at the truth. With enough views, you will eventually be able to see what they all share and the things they disagree on. From this we can remove the points of truth that are only true from a single point of view and then focus on the truths that all the views share. That is the moment we can begin to remove the shaders and begin to look at and study the truth itself without bias. It is the perception of non perception. To remove the experiences that blind us to the truth so we can see the truth unobstructed. It is in this place that we remove the "self" and its perceptions so that we can study and learn truth as our journey doesn't end here, but begins here. We have simply removed the shackles that bind us so now we can pursue actual truth.

Many bring up Bruce Lee's famous quote, "Take what is useful, discard what is useless." But this quote is flawed as who are we to decide what is useful and useless. Some may have passed on martial practices while the next generation may look at it with disgust. But those arts survived to make it to this point, so who are we to say it is useless. One may try one technique and it may not work while trying another that does. That person may say the former technique is worthless while the latter is good. But there are many things to consider. If it didn't work for you, why didn't it work for you? Did you screw up during the technique? Did the situation change and call for a different solution? Did we spend enough time training the technique in question? Don't just throw it away because you may not understand it. It is those techniques that we don't immediately see a benefit to that provide the most benefit as it causes you to have to think deeper about it and practice more. If you already know everything, then why go to learn in the first place?

On the other hand, If a technique goes right, why? Was my technique done correctly, or did I use my superior strength and speed to force it to happen? The compensation will cause problems in the future when there is someone faster and stronger than myself. Did my opponent just happen to be caught off guard? Was it a fluke? Always remember that experiences are not the truth, but they point at the truth. One may not get the technique to work and they may think the truth is that the technique does not work. The failure to apply the technique has revealed a truth, but it may not be the truth you see at first. Perhaps the truth that was revealed was that you didn't spend enough time in practice and thus it failed. Always second guess and ask if the perceived truth I believe is the actual truth.

This is a difficult concept to grasp. People's personal experiences create their personal beliefs and questioning those experiences then questions those beliefs. One must be ready to confront themselves when taking this path. Or they can believe their own house of perceived truths. Living in such a way to protect their ways and reject others all to protect one's own self-delusion. Both ways are hard. We must choose our hard.

Buddhist Thought

To start with a foundation for Buddhist thought in order to more easily understand the chapters to follow, I will list the "4 Noble Truths" below as they are the foundational thought behind Buddhism.

1. *In life, there is suffering.*
2. *These sufferings are caused by attachments.*
3. *You don't have to continue suffering.*
4. *You can end suffering by removing attachments.*

Letting Go of Attachments

The further one goes down any path, the more they will realize that they are the source of most of their own suffering. There may be outside influences that affect things, but even that suffering stems from our own attachments. Some may bully us and try to ruin our reputations, but that only affects us if we are attached to our reputation to begin with. If we don't care how others perceive us, then a bad reputation does not stop us. Attachments cause suffering. Thus we suffer by the things we choose to attach to. If we attach to a sentimental object, we will suffer when something happens to said object. The true way to free ourselves from suffering is to remove attachments.

This all does not mean that attachments are bad and that all people should remove attachments. It simply means that we will suffer from the attachments we make, and we must be ready for that. My older Kung Fu brother whom I respect dearly who grew up with a Tibetan monk refugee in his bedroom was once asked how he can say such things about attachments and yet willingly create attachments by getting married and having children. He responded saying that attachments were like a contract that you sign. You sign these contracts knowing that you will suffer for these attachments, but you also acknowledge that such sufferings were worth it for the goodness one will receive in return. That means that though attachments cause suffering, they are not necessarily bad things. But rather we can accept the terms of suffering in exchange for something we are receiving. If you wish not to suffer, you can work towards removing all attachments. If you wish to make attachments, do so acknowledging and accepting that one will suffer in return. With any relationship, one will experience good times, arguments, times of joy, times of sorrow, times of loss when the things we are attached to are gone or broken. This is the contract of attachments.

The important thing to acknowledge is that we are ultimately the ones deciding why and how we will suffer. If we cannot deal with the suffering that comes, we can choose not to attach. If we find the attachments are worth suffering for, then we can choose to suffer in exchange. So long as we realize that it is our own choice to do so.

Martial Arts is no different than any other road. There will be suffering that is self caused. Some may be worth it, others may simply hold us back and stop our growth. Much of martial arts is actually learning to let go of attachments. We must first let go of the idea that we already know what we are doing and humble ourselves in order to learn the way. This is letting go of our self image in a way. I can't tell you how many people I have met that quit early because "they weren't skilled enough to do the practice." But we must acknowledge that it is through practice that we become skilled. To quit for such reasons means that their self image was being questioned. They may not have liked looking like a fool during the practice, but we can all acknowledge that anyone will look like a fool trying something new. Their self didn't match the image of themselves in their head and it challenged their views of themselves. To protect their self image, they run from the thing they perceive will harm it. In any practice, this is the first wall of their own ego they must break down, but it is not an easy task.

The ego will continue to manifest like this in many more ways along the way. Like with bodily tensegrity in martial practice. We call this example, "feeling our own strength." When we flex and tense our muscles, we tend to "feel" our own strength, but in doing so we actually hold back our own strength. If I were to tense my whole body and attempt to move, it would be slow and stiff. It would also raise our center of gravity as we essentially hold up our weight. Like a baby when it is awake versus asleep. It is perceived as heavier when it is asleep as the baby now is dead weight. In learning to relax we will be able to move freely and faster, and our weight wouldn't be held back. Mass times Acceleration=Force. In relaxing we increase the mass that will be used as well as increase the acceleration. Thus our force will increase. In this relaxation, we will no longer feel the strength of our muscles like before, but that's because we are no longer letting the muscles fight themselves and instead all of the force is given to the opponent. This is again letting go of ego. The ego manifesting in vanity of needing to feel one's own strength. In doing so, we hold ourselves back, in letting go we give the force completely to the opponent. Like a new boss who is experiencing power for the first time. They may abuse their power. Their workforce may diminish from people quitting and others will lose morale. Company profits will suffer. But a good boss who doesn't abuse power is respected by their workforce and they all work together to achieve their goals.

Many in their martial journeys may find themselves in moments of frustration. They might find themselves demotivated. It is important to realize for even the experienced veteran, this is a common dilemma. Whether one realizes it or not, this is their ego desperately trying to hold on and get their attention. The ego is like a nagging monkey in a cage. It will try harder and harder to get your attention the more it gets ignored. The better we get, the louder it will scream. We must realize these moments are desperate attempts of the ego to take control again. Our desire to get better at martial arts will hold us back. For when we desire, we will suffer for it. This desire will create attachments. These attachments will cement us in place along the road. Truly the best thing one can do at this point to improve their martial arts is to stop "trying" to be good at martial arts. This does not mean stop practicing. But rather it means to continue to work, but don't attach to an end goal. Don't attach to waypoints. Instead, continue to walk the path. Not looking back and not looking too far forward, except to look for where to go. Instead, enjoy the moment.

To end this section, I'd first like to address what may appear as hypocritical if left unsaid. Attachments cause suffering. Remove attachments to remove suffering. But one must also realize that in adhering to the thought of removing attachments, one forms a new attachment. Attaching to non-attachment. For the ways we choose to free ourselves can chain us just as hard. It is important then to look back and remember that attachments are a contract. We can choose to suffer in exchange for something we may find worthwhile. In this case we can see the practice of martial arts to be an attachment as well. But it is only a bad attachment if we trap ourselves in it. For example, we have talked about "eating bitter" in the previous chapters. It may seem counterproductive, however sometimes we must create attachments in order to truly remove them. We can only drop a pencil once we have picked it up. Martial arts is one way to enlightenment. So to learn the process of letting go, we must first adhere to a practice that will teach us to let go. We go through grueling training and suffer many sufferings and we gain skills from it. We willingly go through these sufferings knowing that they will benefit us in the future. In this case, we must understand that we are a part of the human condition and that this process is natural.

However, there is something else to acknowledge from this willing attachment. At some point we must let it go. This does not mean stop practicing. It instead means that we must understand that the way we have been traveling is not the only way. We must learn to determine the difference in the way we have attached ourselves to the way. Understand when the suffering and attachments will be worth the time and when they will shackle us. We see many martial artists claiming their art to be the superior art and their way the superior way, but this is the result of the shackles of attachment. They willingly imprisoned themselves to their beliefs. Such people will halt their growth as their learning opportunities will grow fewer. To let go of the way is to understand that there are many "ways" and thus learning never ends. Dharma is the word used to call the way in Buddhist practice. A good friend of mine once went to a Buddhist retreat and the lead monk said this in response to someone's question. "The only attachment that Buddhists have that Buddha didn't have was the Dharma." It is important to adhere to the way until one becomes trapped by the way. Then we must let go of the way.

Emptiness/No-Thing

      Emptiness/No-thing is something that while one can explain it, one can only truly know it from personal experience. It is much better to realize it through lots of reflection. I will continue to talk about it here, but I will encourage others to try experiencing it for themselves. I will talk about the practices that led me there as well as they may be found useful. When I was learning of this from my teacher and he asked me this question I was supposed to ponder in meditation, I gave an answer the moment he asked it as a way to compare answers both before and after training. He gave me an answer that I did not understand at the time. He told me, "Too much intellect, not enough mind." The best way I can describe this now is that after having experienced the change in perspective, before I was not necessarily incorrect, but my mind was not in the right place. The experience of the change itself was like an eye opening for the first time and seeing what has been in front of me the whole time, but my eyes were shut and I could not see. I could theorize, but not experience. It is like the knowledge of knowing a tiger exists. We have computers nowadays and can watch them from afar. We can study them in such ways and theorize about the existence of the tiger. Even knowing what we can come to know, it pales in comparison to being next to the tiger in person. Assuming the tiger won't eat us on the spot, we can witness the tiger firsthand, feel its fur, witness its demeanor and habits. This is where we can truly understand the tiger is a living breathing creature just like us. Now let us get onto emptiness.

My teacher started me with a basic meditation routine to work towards building a foundation for my mind before starting the emptiness training. Basic meditation practices to start a foundation is really important and should not be overlooked as small mistakes as a result of a lack of foundation can lead thousands of miles away from the path. After some time of that my teacher gave me a Zen koan to ponder in my meditations. Zen koans are essentially paradoxical anecdotes or riddles to show the inadequacy of logical reasoning and to instead start the path toward enlightenment. In short they are questions to ponder that will result in a profound realization. The first one my teacher gave me was as follows. "If I asked you to touch your nose, perhaps you would point to the very tip of your nose. I'd like you to touch your nose and not at its tip. Where do you touch? Where is the line between the tip and not the tip of the nose? You have to look smaller and smaller until you reach the cells. But of course at this level where would the division be between the tip and not the tip. At this level, what is noseness?" He then simplified it for practice to, "Where does the tip of the nose end and the nose begin." That was the point I gave an answer, "If I had to answer now, I would say, what is the tip of a nose or what is a nose? We as humans gave these things definitions, but in reality we are one organism." To this he responds, "No good, try again. Less intellect, more mind."

At that I began my practice with pondering this koan. After days of this practice I came back to my teacher saying, "This was the first time in a long time that I started a training and had no idea why I was doing it or what it would do. Before starting I had several possible answers. Now I am unsure if there is an answer at all. If the question is what is the tip of my nose and what line defines it, my best answer would be, Is there a line at all, and does it matter? Isn't it all more of the same? I guess I went from an intellectual understanding to realizing I don't have an answer."

My teacher responds to me saying, "If there is no thing besides the spaces between the cells of the nose and not nose. All things are like this. Made of more empty space than anything else. Our minds are what interpret this differently. So we live in a state of, it's all space and atoms. It's all physical and real. Both of these are true. Emptiness is not sitting in meditation and spacing out thinking of nothing. It's a focused study of what this place is. Empty space more than anything else. Interpreted by our minds as physical."

He gave me a new question to ponder. "Am I my arm? Am I my emotions? Who is doing my martial practice?" I spent more time pondering these new questions. After days more of pondering and meditating, we came back to discuss once again. For the sake of this chapter not rambling on for too long, I am going to summarize the discussion. The essence of what we discussed is that the thing that is our "self" is not our initial interpretation of ourselves. We are not limited to the physical interpretation of ourselves, but we are also made up of the empty space. We are made up of cells. Between those vibrating cells is empty space. In old Buddhist terminology it was referred to as grains of sand and empty space. And between those cells where the empty space lies is also our "self." We are not only grains of sand, but also the empty space. And from that understanding, we can question where our "selves" end and someone else begins. Or if there is a beginning or end to begin with. If we are cells and emptiness, and they are cells and emptiness, what differentiates their cells and empty space from our own? Is there a differentiation at all?

This Emptiness is what connects all things together. In hurting one, I hurt myself. In removing these boundaries of self, we can see just how many boundaries and walls people create. If I hate one, I hate all including myself. Many have heard about the butterfly effect. It is popular in the discussion of time travel in that one small change can result in a completely changed future. The theory named after the idea of a change as small as stepping on a butterfly can create this change. Just think about it. One person steps on a butterfly. Another person is having a lousy day. Had that butterfly lived, it might have met this person and they might have been in a better mood after witnessing something pretty. But now that person takes their bad mood to the office. The people around the office feel this and they also have a bad mood. Some other person from the office now goes to his car to drive home. They drive home angry and make a bad driving decision that leads to them dying. Now the family of the deceased man is grieving while the other person involved in the crash now has to deal with the trauma of having been involved in someone's death. The person goes to court as a result of the grieving family wanting justice for their loved one. Perhaps the court decides to jail the man. Now that person's life is forever changed as well as both families along with the people at the office that sat next to him every day and now deal with that loss. All these people are unknowingly involved in this chain of cause and effect. I could continue to talk about this theoretical scenario, but the point is made. What this emptiness means is that we are all connected. We as martial artists are connected to the rest of our martial family, we are connected to our teachers, we are connected to the people we get in fights with, and we are connected to all the people that those connections are connected to as well. From this realization as we understand while others are blind to it, we hold responsibilities to always attempt to make good decisions. Especially when we are in positions where we can hurt or seriously mess up people. Everything we do has consequences. Not a single act is kept in isolation.

<u>Removing Duality/All is One</u>

It is very human to want to separate things. This manifests in many ways over history in big ways like racism, sexism, leading to things like genocide, creating walls, war, segregation. This also manifests in smaller ways that are more day to day like people with different interests, different thought patterns, etc. These kinds of things create divide, hate, and suffering. These problems don't come from evil though. Rather they form from confusion. Really all of us living in this reality are just confused. This confusion leads to these misunderstandings. These misunderstandings lead to this unproportionate amount of hate. This confusion is the result of humans believing things to live in duality.

Duality is what creates divide. Referring to the taiji diagram, many people would mistakenly refer to the aspects of yin/yang as a duality. But there is no yin and yang. The taiji diagram is meant to convey that it is "yin/yang." Not two aspects, but the same from different perspectives. Everything is connected and affects each other, because they are not truly different things, but rather one thing. In the yin/yang aspect of dark/bright. It is not dark and bright, but a better way to refer to it is a brightness spectrum. There are times where things are more bright, there are times when it is less bright. The sense of duality is only a human's attempts to contrast and define it. But we can call one thing dark in comparison to another thing. But the thing that was the darker object may be compared as brighter in comparison to yet another object. It is a spectrum of one concept, not two separate objects. The same could be said in comparing people. One person could hold beliefs in one way and another person could hold beliefs in another way. These beliefs could make these people appear to be radically different. However, they are still on the spectrum of humanity. They are one, not separate.

In Buddhism, this concept is taught in the "golden thread." The golden thread is the metaphor that everything in the universe is connected to each other by a gold thread. I'm connected to my friend, my friend is connected to this rock, this rock is connected to that bird, etc. Everything is directly and indirectly connected to everything. Not a single thing exists alone. This concept can be understood simply as cause and effect. In a previous chapter I referred to an example of stepping on a butterfly and that causing a chain reaction leading eventually to people dying. It is the same kind of concept. And with this concept we have affected all things and all things have affected us. Nothing exists on its own, but rather it exists through infinite relationships between things. In order for us to even be born, our parents had to be involved. For us to be raised, people had to be involved. To be fed, we needed to have a relationship to something. This tree happened to live near me and time happened to play out just right that the tree still bears fruit for me to eat. It could have been too old or young to bear fruit, but I was here at the right time. In order for me to pay my bills, I had to get paid from my job that happened to be hiring while I was in need of a job. The hiring manager happened to look upon my application with favor. In the workplace I happened to do a good job because my coworkers and I worked together and our efficiency was increased which led to us getting raises which might have made the difference between paying my bills or coming up short. Walking home from work safely was made possible because it just so happened that some guy who was mugging people on the route home I took happened to get caught minutes before I arrived. I was able to later get a promotion because my employer noticed my earnesty in working which was a taught habit from my parents and it continued because of the support of my friends. These are all examples. They show that nothing exists on their own.

I usually stay away from using the word energy, because it is often used improperly and leads to confusion, however for here it works. Whatever energy you put out will come back to you. If you put out negativity, that negativity will spread to those around you. Those around you will spread it to those around them, so on and so forth. This eventually will make its way back toward you. This is what is referred to as karma. Karma is not some cosmic force, but rather cause and effect. You hurt someone's feelings, that person becomes upset. They leave to go home and escape the situation. They drive unsafely from being upset. They crash and die. We hear about it. We now live with the guilt of having the last thing we said to them being negative. On the other hand, when we treat someone well at the workplace, they become happy. They treat the next person well. Everyone in the workplace is in a better mood and morale increases. Productivity goes up and the boss takes notice. The boss congratulates everyone on a job well done and throws a pizza party. Now you get to enjoy free pizza.

Nothing exists on its own. Everything is connected by this metaphorical golden thread. We are all a part of this karmic cycle of cause and effect. Everything that leaves us comes back to us. This implies the paradox that while everything is different, we are all the same simultaneously. We all exist on the same spectrum. We may appear different, but at the heart of things, we are the same. We and all things are one entity. If one thing is affected, all things are affected. This understanding is the key to seeing the confusion and then learning to grow past it.

All People are One/ Hurting Others Hurts the Self

With the past chapter, we understand that we are made of cells and the empty space between them. In Buddhism, this is described as grains of sand and empty space. We ask ourselves the question of where does our nose begin and end. At a deeper level we can ask ourselves, "Where do I begin and end?" At what point are these cells and empty space considered me, and at what point is it considered "not me?" Where do I end and another begin. On earth we learn of states of matter in the form of solids, liquids, gasses, and plasma. The differences between solids, liquids, and gasses are the way the cells interact with space.

In solids, the molecules are formed in patterns and are held in place by attractive forces. The space between them is smaller than the other forms, but still ever present. In liquids molecules flow easily around each other and it maintains its form again through attractive forces. There is more space between molecules than in solids. In gasses the space between molecules is greater. The molecules move between each other at greater speeds and the attractive forces become insignificant.

These are different states of being, yet they are the same object. Water, ice, and steam are an example of the different states of being, yet the components making them up are the same. An object can become different states of being and still be itself, but where is the line in its definition? We exist as cells and empty space, another human exists as cells and empty space, the air between us is cells and empty space. So we are left with the question, Where do we end and another begin, and is there a beginning and end? When looking from the average human perspective it can seem easy to draw lines, but the closer you look into atoms and space, those lines disappear.

The golden thread of Buddhism says that everything is connected and any action affects everything else. This is because through the extension of this idea is that all things are connected as all things are one, not separate things. There are not separate people, but parts of the whole that are just confused about their standing in the world. In Christian ideology, all are referred to as brothers and sisters in Christ. It is further explained as all people make up the body of Christ. Hands and feet, stomach, eyes, etc. All may have different gifts and roles, but are in the end part of a greater whole and make up one being. From this comparison we can see a similar idea.

There are no defining lines except that which we ourselves put there. We are the ones to say, "That is a deer, that is a flower, that is dirt. But it is all cells and empty space. We exist together as one organism. Humans, plants, animals, the earth. We live and breathe together. We all fill our role. Trees provide oxygen for us to breathe, we produce carbon dioxide for them to breathe. Plants produce fruit for us to eat, one day we die and become the soil which becomes nutrients for the plants. It all circles in on itself.

We have probably all heard the saying, "If I hurt you, I hurt myself. With all of this in mind, this becomes both figurative and literal. As martial artists, we must always keep this in mind. As we train, we gain the power to harm others. We must hold ourselves responsible. We must not look at others as separate beings as these divisions allow us to put dissonance between us and them. This dissonance makes us believe it is okay to harm them as there would be no repercussions. Like the dissonance we experience in road rage. Just the fact that we can't see the other person's face who cut us off creates enough dissonance that we act with more passion and anger than we would in a similar situation but in the flesh without the cars. What would we think about the person who cut us off if we sped up alongside them in the other lane to look at their face and then realized it was ourselves in the other car. We must not create these divisions as they will keep us from the path. In hurting others, we also harm ourselves. As others are ourselves, and our selves are others.

Compassion and Selflessness

So we can now start to understand through the last couple chapters why compassion is necessary. If we are all one, we should help each other. As it is said even after meditating in the mountains for years, eventually the Buddha must return to the marketplace. This is essentially saying that now that you understand the way, you must help others who are lost.

It is easy to look at those who demonize us as separate beings and condemn them, but now we know they are the same as us. All people go through loss, all people experience hunger, we all go through good times and bad. Perhaps we now are far better off after much practice and can see things more clearly, but we can all remember what it was like to go through life before we were better off. We can all remember hating others, creating division, and treating others like garbage. We may be better now, but that doesn't mean those things never happened.

So now we can look at those trapped in cycles of hatred, suffering from their countless attachments. We look at them and see ourselves. We see that version of ourself suffering. No person on this earth is purely good or evil. There are circumstances in all of our lives that lead us to where we end up. There are options to help us out of our suffering, but any of those that have gone through the training to reverse this downward spiral knows of its overwhelming difficulty.

So we must have compassion for those that are lost. There are no good and evil people, just those that have worked to see their flaws and now walk the path to do better, and those that are lost and confused.

I think we all can agree that harboring hatred is not a thing a sane person should be doing. Hatred only leads to bad things like revenge, spite, anger. These things are like acid to our body. If someone is harboring these things in them, they must certainly be confused as they are doing themselves great harm. We must look at these people who are lost and confused and see ourselves in them. That part of us that was lost and confused, looking for a miracle. We must help them in any way we can. It is said, "Before enlightenment, chop wood and carry water. After enlightenment, chop wood and carry water." Enlightenment is not something that makes anyone special, nor gives us a higher purpose. It is simply being awake and seeing the thing that's been staring us dead in the face the entire time, but we were blind to seeing it before. Enlightenment is like removing the colored bifocals and seeing the world and its real colors for the first time. Nothing changes, we just now know.

But now that we know, it gives us the opportunity. You go about life as before, but now you see what others are blind to. It is preferable then to use this sight to then go through life and help others along the way. It does not make us righteous. It simply provides us the opportunity to help others in ways we didn't know were needed before. And in doing so, you can help them in the direction towards this same realization. Then they can begin to help others as you are. With this spreading of compassion and love, it can reach the whole world in time.

In the martial arts world this can manifest itself in many ways. But now we can perhaps see that mugger in a new light. Perhaps that mugger is falling on hard times. He may have a family to feed and his job doesn't pay enough to support them. Perhaps the job market is poor and he can't find another job. Maybe this is his first time mugging and you are his first victim. He may put on a scary face, but underneath he may be in tears for what he is resorting to to live. Perhaps just giving him your wallet is both the safest and most compassionate thing you can do. This does not mean you let people walk all over you. There are the three aspects of the Buddha. One of these represents wisdom, another compassion, the third is Vajrapani. Vajirapani is the demon depicted Buddha. Vajirapani is the side that says some demons simply must be slain. In some circumstances the most compassionate thing you can do for someone is put them out of their misery. For example a psychotic serial killer is likely too far gone to walk the path, the most compassionate thing to do for him and his other potential victims is to end the misery. This provides us with difficult opportunities. Some demons need slaying, but not all need slaying. We must always consider and ponder what the most compassionate act is in any scenario. It is difficult to figure out how to respond to a scenario, but I always keep one quote close to my heart when I consider such things. "Violence is never the answer, but when violence is the answer, there is no other answer."

The Many Paths to Enlightenment

One more thing to mention in this section is the many paths to enlightenment. Enlightenment does not have only one path, but many. As stated before, "the only attachment Buddhists have more than the Buddha is the Dharma." It is important to remember not to miss the forest for the trees. The path itself is not enlightenment, but you can find enlightenment through every good path. This does not mean no matter where you go or what you do, you will reach enlightenment. The path to enlightenment is treacherous and difficult. Few will make it in their lifetime. And while there are many ways to enlightenment, there are certainly wrong paths as well that will lead thousands of miles in the wrong direction. But what it does mean is that there are many different paths that all lead to the same destination. Whether we can see it in the moment or not, someone seemingly on a different path may meet us at the destination.

Just in this book alone, we have compared the teachings of Buddhism and martial arts and have seen for ourselves that they tread towards the same end. But it doesn't stop there. Whether you pursue the highest level of cooking, carpentry, painting, it all leads to enlightenment. I once discussed with an artist about the higher levels of art and compared it to martial arts. They said, "First you must follow the rules to learn the foundations of the way. Then you start to follow different styles of art to understand where the higher level artists begin to forge their path and where they start to break the rules in their own way. After that they begin to break the rules themselves and start to let themselves become the painting. To express one's feelings onto the canvas. The highest level then is the removal of themselves as they become a conduit for the portrait to realize itself. You become a tool, and the canvas already knows what it wants to be. You just help them realize it." They then quoted a sculptor who said, "I see the sculpture trapped within the marble. I chip away at it and free it from the marble."

In martial arts we do the same. We learn rules and foundations to build a base. Then we emulate our teachers and masters of the art to learn the principles. Eventually our art has been taken to a stage that we stop emulating as we already have learned the principles. Our bodies and minds transform our art which becomes an expression of our very being. Eventually with enough practice we let go of any style or expression and let the principles of the art express themselves as we become the conduit and we watch our practice as if we are observing ourselves through film. At this point we aren't doing any style, but "the art" is expressed as we move.

In Buddhism they lay down all the foundations. Talk of the 4 noble truths, the rules given to the monks like celibacy, not eating meat. All of this foundation is laid to build off of later. Then the monks emulate the senior monks to further enforce their new lifestyle. They learn how to let go of attachments through the help of senior monks. Then letting go truly starts happening. Emulation is no longer needed and they start to be an example for the next generation. This is the point where they stop from simply being told what to do and they actually start to think about things themselves. Rules are no longer rules, but guidelines. Before, rules are restricting, but now they are the way of life. No longer mindless rules, but now you understand why they are there and how they help you on the path. Finally, they let go of their last attachments. Their attachments to "self." They become the conduit for that they practice. This is emptiness. All good paths lead to emptiness and return to the center.

It is important for us martial artists to keep this in mind. It is easy to see initial differences among styles and that creates barriers and arguments between practitioners. If we walk down the path long enough we will meet everyone at the same destination. If we can see only differences among us, then the chances are we haven't traveled far enough down the path to see the truth yet. Keep going. With time, hard practice and a good mindset, those similarities will make themselves known. It is then that we can look towards each other and mutually work towards our shared goal. When we find true emptiness, there will be no choice but for the walls to come down and we will look each other in the face and see ourselves. At the end of the way, we will be left with no way. But this "no way" is in fact "the way." After traveling "a" way for so long, at the end we will find "no way" and make that our "way." But until then we must travel "a" way. And another will travel "another way," which will lead to the same, "no way." So until we find the "no way," let us help each other as we each travel "a" way so that we can then together find and travel, "the way of no way."

Passing Thoughts

Neigong

Neigong is a term translated directly as "inside work." So inner work or internal work. Many get this term confused with Qigong. Qigong is often translated as energy work. Though the word "energy" doesn't fully describe the concept. Chinese is a very contextual language, so the context can change the meanings of words. As well, English and Chinese languages don't translate well one to one. So early translations of words that were popularized were often wrong or misleading as the word used as a translation could not fully convey the meaning. So for the word Qi, I will refer to its translation as "relationships" as though in some contexts Qi does in fact refer to energy, not all contexts for it mean energy. But "relationships," referring to interactions and effects of things relating to each other can result in energy. In short, not all Qi is energy, but all energy comes from some sort of relationship.

Neigong and Qigong practices and theory can seem the same at a glance as the external look of the practices can even at times look identical, but the purpose of the practices and the goals show their differences. To quote my teacher's sworn Kung fu brother Kevin Wallbridge, Qigong corrects flaws in your structure, while Neigong corrects flaws in your character. Now things can start to make sense. When you look at your flesh as external, many look at Qi (in this context, energy/bioelectricity), something happening inside your body as the internal. However this energy becomes external by comparison if we change the thing we are comparing it to. You can't go much deeper inside yourself than your actual character. From that point of view, energy is more an external expression of internal. All this being said, many may be wondering, "If Neigong is work on your character, what does it have to do with martial practice? Why is it looked upon as advanced martial practice?" One can certainly look at it and say, it is to temper oneself. After becoming a warrior, one must temper themselves to not become a danger to those around them. It can be looked at as gun safety practice. Good people won't hand you a gun if they think you are dangerous. So this character work is essentially, "Sheathing the sword." One would be correct in thinking this is the purpose of Neigong, however it actually has more to do with martial practice than that alone.

Neigong actually improves one's connectedness, power, flow within martial practice. The reason for this becomes more known after considering that the mind and body are not two separate things, but actually two aspects of one thing, yin/yang. The mind affects the body and vice versa. For example, when we are sad or fearful, look at what happens to the body. The chest concaves, the shoulders round, the eyes gaze downwards, almost as if the body is trying to eat itself to escape the situation. When angry, the chest expands, we look forward, we puff up our bodies. Essentially the opposite to the first. With sadness, the chest tightens and the back expands, with anger it is reversed. These are examples of the mind affecting and changing the body. Likewise we can reverse engineer these. We can concave the chest, gaze downwards, and our body which remembers this position will remember the emotions associated with it. It is far easier to be depressed when this is where our body is at. It's like setting the mood. You dim the lights, put out some nice fragrance and soft music and suddenly one's partner finds it much easier to be in the mood.

   With this we see the mind and body are interconnected and not separate. So from this we can extrapolate that a calm and uninterrupted mind is better suited for practice while an emotionally disturbed mind can interfere. Emotional influence causes tightness within the body, which is counterproductive as in martial arts we are taught to relax so that power can flow without interruption. Though not only is this important for "in the moment" emotional disturbances, but also it relates to deeply embedded trauma. With chiropractors and deep tissue massages, it is actually commonplace to have the therapy done and experience emotional disturbances during the treatment. Again the mind and body are interwoven. Through our life we go through much trauma. This trauma results in tightened tissue. It imbeds itself within the tissue as well. Upon having that tissue released, the trauma is allowed to come to the surface. This then allows us to deal with this trauma, or ignore it allowing it to imbed itself once again and tighten up our bodies. By dealing with the trauma, the underlying cause of the tension is relieved, allowing us an extra layer of relaxedness for which we can now improve our practice with.

The practice itself is crucial, but very difficult. That is why it is considered advanced. Learning to punch and kick is easy. Learning to face, deal with, and let go of deeply embedded trauma is difficult. Much like it is easier to cut people out of our lives than it is to forgive. This being said, not all trauma is obvious or even perceived as bad at first glance. We all go through trauma in our lives, but not all of it is regarded as emotional disturbance. Some of it we don't even know exist. Some of it we even mistake for our very "self."

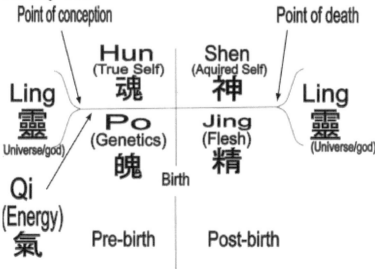

This Chart above is an old traditional chart that illustrates life and death. The Ling(far right and far left on the chart) refers to "the everything" or the universe. The character can be broken into three parts (雨), (口口口), (巫). The first depicts rainclouds. The second is three mouths together which usually is used to depict singing. The third is Wu or Shaman. To be more specific, the character depicts the word ren (人) which means person, twice with something in between them. This illustrates someone living on both sides of the veil. Someone who lives beyond duality. With reference to the shaman aspect it depicts someone who lives on both sides of life and death or someone perhaps that can communicate with the dead. Lots of meanings and interpretations based on context. When depicted together it shows a shaman singing to the sky and praying for rain. The character Ling is referring to specifically what the shaman is singing to. One can interpret this as the sky, the universe, or god depending on what one believes.

The line in the center depicts the moment we are born. Then the side on the left is pre heaven or before seeing the sky(pre birth) while the left is post heaven(after birth). Thus the Ling on the right is the place we come from and the line that starts there and moves towards the central line is when we are in the womb. The line moving towards Ling after the moment of birth depicts our lifespan post birth. Then the moment the line ends is our death with which we return to Ling. We come from Ling and return to Ling. The top left corner is where we see the Hun. The Hun is our "true self." The Hun is the self we are before we are born and influenced by the outside. The bottom left is the Po. It is our body makeup that is decided before we are born. Our genetics. That which we receive from our parents. The top right is the Shen. The Shen is our acquired self. The part of us that is influenced by the world and others around us. The bottom right is the Jing or our body. Our body makeup that we can influence. We can eat healthy and build good Jing or not exercise and build stagnant Jing.

What this chart illustrates for us is that before we are born, we are our true selves, then after we are born we are messed up and changed by everything we interact with. There are big obvious examples of such traumas like experiencing war and then having prejudice against a certain race because when you last saw people of that race they were killing your friends. Such prejudices are introduced by trauma. When we are small children, we don't have these walls. But with experience comes these changes. Smaller examples are less seen. Like someone who is coddled their whole life as a child that then later in life is unable to make decisions or do much as everything was done for them during the years they were learning. One can become something because the trauma they experience has led them there. Everyone goes through this. No one is their true selves, but they are that which they acquire and add to themselves over time. The problem is when you tell yourself something long enough, you will eventually believe it even if you made it up as a lie.

To bring it back to Daoist thought for a minute, much of the practice is recognizing that which is not a part of ourselves, finding the root of which it came from, and peeling off that layer. Continuing to do so until they are their "true self." This process is through the practice of Neigong. Neigong truly is finding the trauma and habits that we have and removing them. In doing so we can peel the layers back and look at our true selves. The "true self" is not actually gone, but rather it is the "conscious observer" of your life. It is watching our lives like a television set while our acquired self runs the show. In meditation we refer to the "monkey mind" that serves to distract us from our practice. This is the acquired self. In meditation we attempt to quiet the acquired self to allow the true self time to exist and breathe. But because the acquired self who normally gets to run the show gets ignored, it tries to get your attention. The more we practice the closer we get to our true self.

Now to discuss the guidelines of Neigong practice. While the specific external practices may vary from person to person, the route is essentially the same.

1. *Move the four big joints*

The four joints refer to the shoulders and hips. The general idea is essentially trying to follow nature in fundamental ways. When one is without motion, they die. Even while we rest, blood moves, heart pumps, the mind works. So we must help promote that movement so that we can live better lives. The four big joints are also the closest to the torso where all the tissue that typically carries trauma lies. To move those helps to loosen the tissue to release trauma. And in moving the four joints the others get exercised as well. This practice helps to root you in your flesh.

2. Learn to Stand

This practice typically involves standing meditations of some kind. The practice here is to change your reflection of yourself by finding where you stand in the universe, literally. Here we connect ourselves to where we are in space. It is a practice of reflection.

3. Finding the Earth

This is figuring out where we are. The more we stand, the more comfortable in standing we become. So we can relax about where we are and find the earth for which we are on. Releasing the upper body through the lower body as you breathe. We settle, we sink. This is a practice of grounding ourselves in reality.

4. How we Manipulate the Universe

Picking up things, touching people, moving objects. Like a child reaching and grabbing things trying to learn. When they find something new, they become obsessed and try again. Through practice we learn how touching people also touches their mind. Like how a hand on the shoulder can create warmth and comfort to someone who is grieving. This is a practice of how our interactions with things affect them. And how those interactions affect things down the line.

5. Action/Non-Action

Putting the mind in the present moment. Not thinking about the end result. Not striving, yet leaving nothing undone. It is not the idea of thoughtless action, nor doing nothing. It is discussed prior about learning how actions affect others. Rather it is a practice of living in the present moment. Not getting caught up in the past nor worrying for the future. Living in the only moment that truly exists at any given time. The "here and now." Doing the work of today while not concerning oneself with trying to be some great warrior or Ceo in the future, but focusing instead on the path before us right now. No one becomes Ceo by worrying about the end goal. Instead they focus on the path they are walking which will bring them to such a position.

From this we can extrapolate that the first three points are about observing and finding your "self." The last two are about how you interact with what is around you. With these as guidelines for practice, you should be able to learn from any qualified teacher and practice their method of Neigong and find the benefits. Peeling back the layers of things added by others to find the conscious observer (true self"). Otherwise we become a puppet of the acquired self. The acquired self is not who we are. It is what we convince ourselves we are. It is like when we try to change our personality to fit in with a friend group. We try to portray ourselves as something to convince them that we fit. With enough lies, we will eventually convince ourselves with these same lies. Eventually we won't be able to even separate the lies from the truth. Our true selves and the "self" we portray will not match and this leads to identity issues. Not only that but we will eventually be so deep into our trauma that it will look impossible to climb out, leading to a complacency among the lies. This is the hard work that no one wants to do, but that is why it is worth doing. The things that are truly worth it are not easy fixes, but years of hard work. But the hard work is worth it.

Change is Constant like the Tides

(Modern Taiji Symbol)   (Bagua Diagram)

The concept of change is paramount to martial arts and everything. One must change and adapt to the times and situation or they will always be a step behind. In old times failure to adapt meant death and the failure to pass on one's bloodline. Not as extreme of examples today, but the concept is still clearly true. Failure to adapt to technology leaves one in a less desirable and applicable market when looking for a job. Failure to adapt to changes in supply and demand means the failure of a business. Failure to adapt to someone's tactics in a fight can lead to losing the fight and dying if it was a serious conflict.

Thus the need to adapt is established. Several martial systems were built on this very premise. BaguaZhang, the martial art based around the concept of the Bagua which is a diagram for telling about change and predicting the patterns of change. Ma family Kung Fu which is also based around the Bagua concept(diagram, not the style). Taijiquan which is based around the Taiji symbol(yin/yang) and the concept of yin/yang interchange. The concept is both simple and complex depending on how you look at it. I will try to keep things simple.

When taking the scenario of an attacker, we meet them in combat and we are generally met with two possible outcomes. The current me(current strategy) is enough to stop the opponent, or the current me is not able to stop the opponent. When the first possibility is the truth, then you simply continue on the path and victory is assured. When met with the second possibility, we must either change and adapt or die. The three martial arts I mentioned take this literally. To use the Ma family kung fu as my current example, each subsystem in it comes with its own strategies. For example, monkey style likes to grapple and takedown, Long fist likes to strike with heavy fists. When one approaches the combat scenario with Long fist as their strategy, things may go south if the range closes into grappling range. At that point, the practitioner must change their strategy to best suit the situation. In this case switching to monkey grappling strategies may be advantageous. On the other hand if the conflict gains some space into striking range, the practitioner may want to switch to Long fist to take advantage of the striking range.

In Taijiquan, it is looked at as different energies rather than styles. For the main strategy, the practitioner will employ the 4 primary energies of Peng, Lu, Ji, and An(Expand, lead to emptiness, squeeze out of the space, load release). These 4 can be summed up as the practitioner becomes an overwhelming force. With the expansive force it makes it impossible to take their space. Every time one attempts to touch them, their force falls on emptiness. However not all conflicts are easy, thus the secondary energies come into play. Cai, Lie, Zhou, Kao(plucking, splitting, elbow, body attack). These energies are reserved for desperation moments and enemies who won't go down easily. Plucking the opponent to forcefully unbalance them, striking them with elbow strikes which are dangerous strikes. It all teaches change.

Baguazhang looks and is known as an art of circular movement, but while the circular movement does indeed exist in Baguazhang, it would be more accurate to say Baguazhang is the art of change. Its footwork alone assists this idea as the footwork is quick, continuous and never stopping. Baguazhang is also known for its palm changes(essentially short repeating forms or drills). Each palm change represents one of the eight trigrams and thus a change for itself. Each change will represent a change in tactics as well as a change in body type(how one carries and uses the body). In one moment one will have a solid lower half to knock into the opponent causing them to fall. Another moment the lower half will be light allowing for fast footwork and a hasty retreat. Retreating to attack again. Feigning high to attack low. The list of changes are endless. We are left with the idea, when a force becomes overwhelming, we must change. We must adapt or fall.

In life, we must adapt. Whether big or small. Change is not a binary thing. There is not a moment of change, but rather change is like the waves on a beach. Constant, flowing, rising, falling, gradual change happening over periods of time. One must always look to better and improve oneself in this way. Not because you have no other choice, but because the moment we stop, growth stops too. Everyone has met that one guy they knew some time ago and they meet in recent times only to see their mentality hasn't changed in the slightest. Change is natural. We must change, or we will fall behind. This doesn't mean we change ourselves to become another person, but instead to constantly chip away at the layers interfering with us. Like in Science discoveries, it is always changing. This is not because scientists are dumb, but because they recieve new information that may make their previous hypothesis to be incorrect. So they look again at the new evidence and create a new hypothesis. Only a fool would continue to fight for the theory that was outdated or proven wrong. One must look at all the current evidence, and follow that to create a new hypothesis, and not attach to that hypothesis so as not to be at a loss when it is proven wrong.

Just with any other thing, we can't do the same thing over and over and expect a different result. When looking for a romantic partner, one can try the same dumb pick up line over and over and fail every time. Perhaps it is time for a different strategy.

In life we are met with many waves of change. One can try to swim against these waves, but they will find a difficult and tiring life. It can even spiral to the point where turning one's life around at that point can seem unfeasible as they are so far gone and have much change they must go through. Thus it is important to change as change comes our way. Though it is not too late for those far gone. The fact that we are alive means it's not too late. The mountain of self-work that must be accomplished may seem impossible, but it is certainly possible. Don't look at the mountain in front of you lest you be discouraged. Instead look at the small mound of dirt in front of you and start with that. Some mounds may be bigger than others and may seem like mountains themselves. But if you do a little at a time, those mounds become smaller and smaller. Don't look up at the mountain, look ahead and work on the mound. Little by little, change by change. You will be transformed.

Present Moment

When one is trapped in the past, the road ahead becomes hazy and filled with obstacles. When one gets caught up with thoughts of the future, they can lose sight of the direction they are headed. Both are pitfalls and both are lies. The past and the future don't truly exist in the way we think they do. The only thing that really exists at any given time is the present moment.

The more we get stuck in the past, the more regret will latch onto us. Living in the past is the path of depression. Regret, shame, weakness, doubt, these are all things that come when we compare ourselves to the past. Regret can only exist because there is something to regret. Regret by its very nature is wanting to take back something that is already done. Shame is regret for the judgment of something that is done. The feeling of weakness wouldn't be called weakness if it wasn't compared to something. If in the past we felt good, but now we feel weak comparatively, we would call ourselves weak. But if we didn't have that stronger feeling in the past, this weak feeling would just be normal. Doubt comes along when we no longer have belief in ourselves. But again it is always in comparison with a time in our lives when we weren't in doubt.

The more we dwell on the past, the more it drags on the current moment. And though the past may have existed at some point, it no longer exists at all in reality. The only place it exists is in our memories. The present moment is not the past. What is done in the past is done. We cannot go back. We cannot change it. With depression, we are essentially in the middle of an identity crisis. We cannot separate our past selves from our present selves. When one is depressed from bullying that happened in school and are now grown adults, we are no longer that bullied child. Yet we can still be dragged down by those painful memories and have self-doubt because of it. But we must remember, we are no longer that child. Even if we are put in the same situation years later, we will never react or respond in the same way we did in the past. We are different people now. That person we were as a child no longer exists. There is only our present moment. We are no longer a helpless child being bullied by other helpless children. We are grown adults at this point. Would we as adults be bothered the same way by children attempting to bully us as we were then? As an adult we get a new perspective and we have made some way into the world now. At times it may not seem like we've come that far, but that is again because we are confused about who we are and what time it is. Remember, the past is done. We are different people.

Just as there are dwellings of the past that inhibit us, there are inhibitions of the future as well. We usually refer to this as anxiety. Living in the future. This kind of living is also unhealthy. By living in the future, it creates many possible scenarios for any given situation. More than likely none of the given scenarios will even happen. We fret over the ten thousand things, but we miss the present, which is the only moment that exists. Even if we happen to guess what will happen by mere chance, it doesn't do us any good. It would have happened regardless, but now we are stressed out about it because we couldn't let go of the many possible outcomes. The nervousness created from the anxiety can even be debilitating leading to no action through inability to act or indecision. This then makes us miss out on what was waiting for us.

But the future doesn't exist. We cannot see the future, nor experience it. Even if we were to make a correct guess about future events, the time we will experience them is the present. We must remember this, or we will debilitate ourselves before any events could happen. Most of our suffering is self-caused. One may say that if we aren't focused on the future, we won't get anywhere. But actually if you are focused on the future, then getting nowhere is the only certainty. The only way to walk the path is by focusing on the path we are walking which only exists in the present moment. If we look too far ahead on the trail, we'll surely miss the signs directing us as well as we will miss the signs warning us for bears. If we take for example one person's journey to become Ceo at their company, if they are so focused on becoming the Ceo, their attention won't be fully focused on the work in front of them. Their work will be sloppy and other people will be considered for promotions instead. So the worker must focus on the work in front of them.

One can't make it to the finish line until they've run the race.

The only moment that exists is right now. The past will never be "right now." The future will one day be "right now," but only when it is "right now." Thus it won't be the future anymore. All this is easier said than done as many people suffer these things and never even know it. So I will leave this chapter with a saying my teacher gave me to ask myself whenever depression, thoughts of the past, or anxiety, thoughts of the future become overwhelming. The Question: "Where am I? What time is it?" The Answer: "I'm right here. And it's right now."

Simply Sitting

There is so much going on around us on any given day. As technology advances, life moves at a faster pace. More is expected of us by our bosses, many of us cannot take a single moment to chill. People try to fill each and every second of their lives. Not taking breaks, only doing and completing their tasks. Going to bed only to wake up and do it again. This is a good way to let life pass you by. The faster one goes, the faster the end comes. Without taking time to stop and smell the roses we find ourselves at the end of our lives. We cling to life, for we feel unfulfilled. Spending our lives to make the future better, but now we have no future left. We missed the present completely. All this can be fixed ahead of time by dedicating time everyday to the simple practice of sitting.

Meditation comes in many forms from laying down to standing to walking, but one of the more popular is sitting. Many would ask as to how sitting and meditating can benefit a person. Think about all the thoughts that go through your head in a day, or maybe an hour, maybe even a single minute. Especially with the way society is set up today, for many they can't count the thoughts. The practice of meditation is a dedicated period of time where we narrow those thoughts down to 1 or 2. Perhaps on a specific thought. The practice has even been used by monks in old times to memorize scriptures.

Many don't realize just how much blood and energy the brain uses on a daily basis. On average it consumes 15% of total oxygen from the blood of the entire body. That's more than any other part. It makes more sense when knowing this as to why spending all day at the office drains someone's energy even though they were sitting most of the day. Not to mention lethargy. Just like the body needs rest, the mind needs rest too. They aren't really two different things.

Meditation also gives us a real look into our mind and how it functions. Shen (神) is a term usually translated as spirit, but contextually here it refers to the mind. The Shen is broken into 3 parts. Xin (心), Yi (意), and Zhi (志). Xin means heart and refers to the emotional mind. The part of yourself that feels emotion. The more creative part of yourself. Yi means intent and refers to the intellectual mind. The part of yourself that looks at and analyzes things. Zhi means willpower or drive. The part of your mind that pushes you. Mind over matter kind of things. When these three work in harmony, you have a strong Shen.

Unfortunately, we have to learn how to keep them in harmony. Usually the Xin and Yi are not made distinct and we are driven by our emotions and ego. When someone cuts us off in traffic, we immediately flare up in anger. This is the Xin taking control. Almost all live in this space to some degree. The way to fix this is to spend time each day to sit. Not sit and watch tv, not sit and play a game. Sitting and nothing else. By taking the time to narrow your thoughts and sit, you give your brain time to rest. This rest means it's not using the same amount of energy as usual and some of it gets saved. Most people spend their mind energy on a deficit and lack real mind power. But by saving a little every day, we build up reserves to be used when needed.

This saving also helps to create space between the Xin and the Yi by creating space, you are making the distinction between the two. It's like putting distance between them. Now when someone cuts you off, instead of immediately reacting in anger, you will see your anger coming from a distance. This gives your Yi a time to reflect on whether or not getting angry is worth the time and energy. Then instead of reacting, you can choose to act. Choose whether it is worth getting angry or not. As an analogy, picture a young couple. This is their first relationship and they are figuring things out. Perhaps the boy wants to make the girl happy, so he acts differently than normal to please her. Being new to relationships, she doesn't catch on that he isn't acting as himself. What she likes, he likes. What she hates, he hates. When she gets mad, he gets mad for her sake. When she cries, he cries for her sake.

This is an unhealthy relationship. Rather than being himself, he becomes what he thinks she wants. He becomes like her and the distinction between them becomes less. This is what the Xin and Yi are like without sitting practice or similar practices. Instead we need them to be distinct so that they can work together. The boy doesn't need to like and hate what she does, but instead respect them while also expressing his own individuality. When she is angry or sad about something, he can remain calm in order to be there for her in what she needs rather than egging her on by becoming a mirror. A healthy relationship can be made when there is some distance. When a couple is too clingy, it hurts both of their individualities and they can not effectively help each other. They also need to be able to spend time apart as themselves.

In the same way, in order to deal with daily tasks and stresses, Xin and Yi need to not cling to each other, but work together. And our Zhi can be trained by the discipline of sitting. There will be days and times where we will not want to sit. It is the training of our Zhi that is the part of our mind to keep us going. Xu Guoming said, "Sit for 20 minutes a day. If you don't have time for it, sit for an hour."

One common mistake in this distancing of the emotions is that people may come to the conclusion that they need to get rid of their emotions. This is incorrect. It is not getting rid of the Xin, but giving distance so that they can work together in harmony. To get rid of Xin is also to get rid of ethics. It is in our heart that we can feel and empathize with others. Empathy guides morals. Logic alone leads to selfishness.

Life is full of many things, good and bad. Always remember through it all to sit and breathe. When conflict becomes too much, sit, breathe, calm down. With your now non-panicked and calm mind reevaluate and resolve the issue. You'd be surprised how many problems can be solved by taking time to simply sit.

Hardships for Training

To start this chapter, first I'd like to list the 7 hardships for martial training.

1. *Experience cold, heat, and rain by scaling high mountains and crossing deep valleys*
2. *Rest in open fields and sleep in the mountains*
3. *Never store money or food and never wear warm clothes*
4. *Travel everywhere to engage in contests*
5. *Reside in graveyards, haunted houses, or among wild beasts*
6. *Associate with dangerous criminals*
7. *Live off the land among peasants*

It is easy to want to live comfortable lives and it is encouraged by today's culture. We progress in technology and build a society in which it takes little effort to do daily tasks that would normally be a chore. Certainly not a wrong thing, however getting used to such things can weaken the generations. As it is said, "Easy times make weak men." When society allows us to live without lifting a finger, then lifting a finger gets seen as a chore. Like with yin/yang, it is always based on the context of the things we are comparing. If we are comparing training for war to moving furniture, training for war would be harder. But if we instead compare moving furniture to pouring a glass of water, moving furniture would obviously be harder. It all depends on the context of what is being compared.

From this we can extrapolate that living in easier times makes normal times seem hard, while hard times makes normal times easy. We can start to understand the lessons the 7 hardships give us. One doesn't necessarily have to follow the list exactly, but the lesson to take back is that one shouldn't seek to only be comfortable. When one only knows comfort, then when life demands from them, it will seem insurmountable. The 7 hardships are to teach us to experience hard times. Because these hard times will make us strong. When one experiences hard times and an insurmountable task comes their way, such a task will not be too difficult as the hardships have become a normal part of life.

Whether we like it or not, no matter how much we try to make life as comfortable as possible, hard times will come upon us. It is up to us to be ready for them when they come. We can try to distract ourselves with comfort and nice things, but when we hide behind these things, they will only come crashing down and we will be unprepared for the task before us.

As martial artists, we prepare for the worst possible outcomes our society has. So why do we train in perfect conditions? Why do we only train on perfectly flat floors? Why do we only train falling and rolling on mats? Why do we train to fight only in an open space? Why do we only train outdoors when the weather is sunny and not rainy? Why do some train only choreographed routines and then expect to handle the chaos of combat. We are not guaranteed these conditions in combat. One may say, "when the bad conditions come, I'll just adjust to them." Such an idea is foolish. The way people train is how they will fight. So instead one should train on uneven ground. Train without mats. Train in areas with many obstacles. Train in poor weather. Spar and prepare for chaotic situations. All these things will prepare us for reality. It does not mean we shouldn't ever enjoy good conditions when they are available, but it does mean we shouldn't intoxicate ourselves on them.

One other take away from these hardships is empathy. Though more widely accepted in today's culture, there are still those who look at empathy as weakness. Empathy is the ability to understand and share the feelings of another. Many still look at this as a show of being weak and letting emotions take control of you, however it is actually the opposite. Empathy is a show of strength. Empathy is the suspension of one's ego to come to understand another human being's point of view and see from their eyes. While empathy may come easier for one person than another, it is also a learned thing. But one thing empathy requires is the experience or the ability to perceive that which we are attempting to empathize with. Without experience it is harder, though still possible. But with personal experience it becomes easier to empathize. And from that one can then learn to empathize without experience.

We may try to empathize with someone who is going through a hard time. This becomes easier after having gone through hard times ourselves. This makes someone who trains under hardships someone who is easily able to empathize with another's hard times. It is easier as they have been there already or are still there. With one who goes through hardships, they understand how difficult those hardships are and will be more empathetic towards those who now go through the same. It is like looking at a mirror and seeing your past self going through the suffering that you have experienced. With such a mentality it becomes more second nature to help them through or support them. Weak men would scold or mock saying, "Look at you suffering. If only you were like me." Such people don't even realize they are looking in the mirror. They forget where they came from. Likely through attempting to forget the trauma, they hide it in themselves and forget they were ever in such hardships. They then have the urge to mock those who go through the same sufferings as their subconscious is trying to hide their pain by inflicting it on others just like a bully. Truly the strong one is the one who admits their hardships and moves to support others.

Life doesn't always go the way we want. So we shouldn't hide from reality. Hardships will come and we shouldn't hide, but face them. Others will come and we shouldn't look at them to say, "at least I'm not like them." For in doing so your subconscious is only trying to hide its pain. Instead we should come to hear them in their moments of hardships. Empathize with

and support them. This is the path of the strong
human.

Return to the Beginning

No matter what we do, no matter how far we go, the foundation we build is what gives us the ability to do and go. We may do martial arts, we may clean, we may cook, we may paint, the foundation is what builds the skills to do these things. We may go far. We may impress people with our skills and ability. But it is the bland basics that allow all the advanced tricks to work. Everything starts and ends with basics.

It is said, "From wuji(no extremity) comes Taiji(grand extremity). From Taiji comes the 10,000 things." This is said in many variants, but the often less said is, "From the 10,000 things reverts to taiji, taiji returns to wuji." Eventually everything comes full circle and returns to the source. Like a lifespan, we come from nothingness and at first life is simple as a child. Things become more complicated as we become adults, but eventually we retire and life returns to simplicity of enjoying time with loved ones, then we die and return to nothingness. From nothingness we are born and to nothingness we return.

In martial arts we always start with the basics. Stances, footwork, basic hand techniques, basic drills and partner work to work on timing. From there we build off of the foundation with more complicated theory, techniques. Learning to string together simple to complex ideas further building off of the simple foundation. In the beginning we start with basic circles. Those circles may be big, small, long and thin, or fat and large. We eventually learn to build off of those circles. Changing the direction of one circle into another without break or stop. These circles become more complex as we perform our movements. A fat circle becomes thin, then changes from horizontal to vertical, then becomes wide. It can get more and more complex with training. This complexity challenges our brains and our bodies. What was once simple is now difficult. Can we still apply our martial principles under more complex movement? This is the time we are challenged and given the opportunity to test if our foundations are solid enough to handle such movements without sacrificing efficient movement principles.

Many stay in this place however. They learn thousands of techniques and hundreds of forms. Further complicating things. Staying here in this stage is like staying a child lost in a candy store. Always looking for that next delicious piece. This is the way of the forms schools. To improve beyond this point, the child must grow into an adult. It does not mean we can no longer enjoy new candy, but the candy can no longer be the thing that controls us. We must return to the foundation. A child's taste palette may always be looking for that next sweet thing, but the adult can appreciate the sweet thing while also learning to appreciate the food that sustains us and builds good health.

At this point we return to our basic circles. The work has been done. We have proven we can handle the more complex circles while maintaining the principles. Now we return to basic circles. All movements are based on circles, so practicing circles fortifies all moves. Practicing and honing horizontal circles practices and hones all circles that fall under the horizontal category. You don't need to practice one thousand techniques to understand one idea anymore, but you can practice that one basic idea and the one thousand variants of the circle will improve as a result. It is said, "I do not fear the ten thousand techniques you practice once, but the one technique you practice ten thousand times." In this case the ten thousand techniques improve because we invest in the one concept that they all share.

We start with stances, footwork, basic hand techniques, and we end there too. In life we start as a child supported by our family. We become adults and try to fend for ourselves. Our family gets older and we tend to them. We return to the foundation as a changed human. We must be careful in all that we do to not get caught up in the ten thousand things that are ever alluring. But to focus on the important base that we stand upon. No house built on a crappy foundation will stand forever. We must tend to it, reinforce it, or be caught up and swept away by the current of the ten thousand things.

Lessons Grow on Trees

There comes a time in our lives where the older generation passes on and we are left as the examples to the next generation. We can use our own knowledge and wisdom to do like our teachers did and pass these things on to those that will come after us. For many their personal journeys end here as they teach the next because they have no more teachers to take them further. In many cases people at this stage will start to believe their own headlines. With no one above to teach them, they get used to the spot at the top. They get comfortable and start to believe this false notion that they've "made it." However, contrary to how it may seem this is not the end to our personal journey, but yet the beginning of a new chapter.

When our teachers pass on, we must come to understand what exactly a teacher is. In our younger years, teachers appear to us as people who have more knowledge than ourselves. We follow these people in attempts to learn what they know. But when those teachers are gone, we must come to realize that teachers don't have to be someone who knows more than us. They don't even have to be people at all. The further we go, the less dividing lines separate things. Our teacher does not have to confine to a particular set of rules, but anything we can learn from is our teacher.

One of my teachers once told me, "In any profession, 20% of people are really skilled in the profession, 80% are average to below average. Being that martial arts is a niche hobby already and getting skilled takes more work than most people will put up with, the ratio is more like 90/10. But 1% of that is where the titans live. The titans tread new ground unseen to the previous generations." If we take a moment to step back, that means that only 10% of martial artists that we meet are worth emulating. Emulating the other 90% would lead to average or poor skills. This leads to another of his quotes. "Everybody sucks, so look at what they do and do the opposite." Certainly not a nice sounding quote, but if we take the concept of what it is pointing at to heart, then we can take and learn from the other 90%.

If 90% of people are average or below, then by looking at them and doing the opposite, we are looking for the things that keep them average and looking at our own practice to ensure that we are not doing them. There are many things to consider that lead to average training. Far too many to list. Some of those situations may result from a poor work ethic or having a poor teacher. From this we learn that having a good teacher is important and that having a good work ethic is essential. We can look at examples of practitioners that have a poorly maintained bodily structure and a high center of gravity and find that said example leads to being easily tossed around. It reminds us to watch our structure and to sink the weight. There are plenty more examples, but for now let's move on.

As we remove the defining lines of what a teacher is, we can also come to realize that teachers don't even have to be human, nor do they have to be living things. This is where we can start to see how martial arts have developed over the centuries. There are many styles of martial arts based on animals and concepts related to animals like the predatory nature of the tiger, the swiftness of birds in flight like cranes, eagles, etc. Such training naturally leads to learning from nature which has led to the creation of many martial styles. In such styles we may even be taught by our teachers different imagery to enhance our practices. Standing solid and rooted like a tree, flowing back and forth like a moving current, float like a butterfly sting like a bee. We can take inspiration from all around us. One can look at a tree and see that it bends and sways in the wind, but it stays upright due to its roots and its bending helping to absorb the forces of the winds. We can then emulate that in practice by lowering our center of gravity and relaxing so as not to be stiff and easily thrown around. We can look at a river and see that while water is soft to touch, a strong force of waves can crumple structures. So in practice we can emulate its ability to bear down like a tidal wave, but also swiftly flow through the cracks of an opponent's defense like the river moving around the rocks.

Ultimately we are the ones to decide when our journey is done. There are the resources around us to continue to learn until the day we pass, but the choice to settle is up to us. In settling, progress stops. It is against nature to stop like this. Change happens everyday. We can continue to adapt, or hide under a rock. Should we hide under a rock, we should be prepared for the consequences of doing so. Upon emerging from the rock, we will see the world has long since passed us by. Having no teacher is no excuse to stop learning. As we have discussed, teachers exist all around us. People, animals, trees, water, the wind, the stars. We can learn from anything should we open ourselves to see it. We must make ourselves open to it. Ultimately we are our own best teacher. Any teacher can only point the way to success, but the student must walk and train in the path. All the work is done by us. All the information our teachers give us, we must spend time teaching ourselves with it. When said teacher is gone, it is the duty of ourselves(the true teacher) to look for a new teacher to teach us. And from those teachings we continue to teach ourselves. Ultimately the key to progress is to understand the yin/yang of teacher/student. We are both our teacher and a student, always willing to keep learning. We must never lose either aspect, or we will lose sight of the path and be lost in the woods. To always remain a student means to always look for the path ahead. To always remain our own teacher is to have a machete to cut down foliage when there is no certain path. To create a new one.

The Self is Reflected on all Things

It is important to remember and understand that all of us suffer. It is one of the truths of this world. There is not a single person that can escape the fact that we are born into this world and will suffer in this world. While we live in this world we will also meet scenarios where there will be others who will attempt to make us suffer. This may appear from our point of view to be malicious. However if we remove our point of view to look at things subjectively, we will eventually find that we are not so different from them.

Let's refer to these people as bullies for clarity of reading. These bullies attempt to harm us whether physically, psychologically, emotionally, but they do this because they suffer too. You can look at it as their attempt to pass on their suffering to you. In their minds they suffer. They simply want to be rid of the suffering. One may think by bringing harm to others, it gives them some sort of control or power in their lives. With this thought pattern they may come to assume that with power and control, they won't suffer anymore. By attempting to exhibit power over another they are trying to remove their suffering and replace it with power. For many they believe with money and power, nothing can make them suffer. Yet money and power often lead to isolation and that creates more suffering. Yet when in the depths of suffering, seeing things logically is often difficult, even seemingly impossible.

In the heat of the moment, it is difficult to see that bringing suffering to others does nothing to elevate us.

Suffering creates a veil over our eyes that makes it hard to see that these horrible acts won't help us. It also makes it difficult to realize that our actions hurt others. Even with direct involvement, when one is in suffering, it is difficult to see beyond the suffering to the greater picture. Such a person will think simply, behave instinctually. Every person passing by is a potential threat to well being. Every helping hand is seen as an attempt to backstab. Like a frightened animal backed into a wall. They'll bite even those trying to help because they are in the heat of the moment at the height of fear. We all want to get out of that corner and from that perspective the way to escape the corner is to fight.

Jealousy is one such way this can manifest. One can look at another with envy, because they believe if they have what the other person has, then they can be happy. But since the bully lacks it while the other possesses it, envy is created. Maybe they can steal it from them and possess it themselves. Or maybe destroy it so no one has it. Such backwards thinking, yet we can see it comes as a result of trauma and fear. Robert Thurman (Childhood friend of the Dalei Lama and studied Buddhism together) once said, "Everyone is just confused," referring to the state of people. It is the confusion that causes suffering. The man who intently works to hurt others so that they can feel better is confused about what brings healing and what aids us in our suffering. True release of suffering comes from within. Letting go of the attachments that bind us. Letting go of the things someone else possesses so as not to suffer from jealousy. Letting go of the need to live a certain way and instead coming to accept and find contentment in what we already have.

Those who are drunk and attempt to harm us are suffering. Drunkenness can reveal the bitterness of one's soul that they normally hide. That bitterness is from suffering. Perhaps it is best to let go of our egos in such a scenario. Accept the rudeness of the man. Know that he is suffering and let him let out his suffering. Not returning his rudeness with fists. Take pity on the jealous man for he is confused and thinks your wealth of possessions will make him whole. Have compassion for the thief for he steals because he suffers. Compassion on these people does not mean accepting the acts or condoning the behavior, rather it means knowing that we all come from a similar place of suffering. One circumstantial difference and the positions could be reversed. Sometimes we need a smack to get us to realize. Sometimes we need a hug. Compassion comes in many forms. But we must avoid acting in spite. Instead choose your actions and reactions from a place of compassion.

Layers and Threads of Trauma

This next chapter comes from a very personal place. It is an analogy that I made to describe what was happening to me at a certain point in my life. I write this because I believe it may be helpful to others, so while I won't give personal details, I will be thorough about the experience.

Dealing with trauma is no easy task. It is not a linear process, rather it is a complicated interwoven tangle of knots. Thus I compare each individual trauma to a thread. When we are hit with trauma, a thread begins. In the moment of trauma, it is creating problems for our future. If we deal with it then, we can let go of it and heal. Like dealing with the loss of a loved one. There is a grieving process. By going through and accepting this process, it guides us to the path of moving on. Or for many they shut it out, deny it, or keep their grieving inside themselves. This leads to problems later on as the trauma embeds itself into their tissue. At that point it creates a thread. That thread gets longer the more they refuse to deal with it. People end up living their entire lives like this and they often forget that the decisions they make now are not their own, but decisions created from that trauma.

Looking back at one's past to attempt to let go when it has already settled is difficult, but it is the right path. One may mistakenly think though that the trauma is one point in their lives and that dealing with that point will deal with the trauma. I would compare this as the threads of trauma in our lives are lined up next to each other, but not touching. One may think if they deal with that moment, they have truly let go. Unfortunately it is not quite that easy. Trauma is not linear but as stated before an entangled web. One cannot simply pull on the end and remove it.

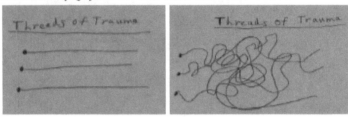

As pictured above, each trauma thread is not in a line, but they tangle and intersect with each other. The point I make in the analogy with these intersection points is that the trauma will interconnect with other trauma and manifest at different points in our life. Every intersection is where the trauma blends together and results in a change. For example, one may grow up an orphan and may develop trauma from loneliness. They may eventually get adopted, however perhaps the adoptive parents are highly abusive. This will create trauma manifesting in trust issues. Later in their life they may find a significant other and may become super clingy as a result of the loneliness and now finally having someone. However the trust issues may cause suspicions of infidelity. Unable to trust their beloved, yet afraid of abandonment. You can see how these trauma will intersect and create problems. Left for too long and it may become paralyzing. Can't leave, because they don't want to be alone. Can't stay, because they lack trust.

     In order to actually deal with trauma, it is a slow process that requires patience. As I dealt through mine. It was like pulling these threads. Eventually I would get to a knot where these trauma manifested and entwined. I would have to spend time with the knot to untangle it. The first step to this is to try to follow the thread to its source. The springing source of the trauma. From there you can come to an understanding of where it came from in the first place. From there begin pulling until you find the first knot. Seeing how this trauma affected and changed you resulting in decisions at that point in your life that you otherwise would have done differently. Come to accept that the past happened the way it did and that you are no longer the same person and trying to change. The knot in time will be untangled, then we continue up the thread to the next knot.

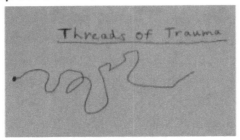

     Eventually you may work all the way through one of the threads. You remove it and then begin to work on the next. Eventually you may notice snowballs rolling down the hill effect. Each time gets a little bit easier. Like the pics above, with each thread gone, there are less intersections and less clutter. You can see more clearly where each thread goes. The intersection points that were there before are no longer there as you have already done work to let go and accept that space. So while there may be a thread that moves through it still, it is no longer the knot it was and the process can get smoother. With each thread removed, you can see more daylight, more hope. Your mind will be in a better place to deal with the rest.

This is a lifelong process, but assuming we manage to remove all of the threads and we remove the "self" that was made as a result of our trauma to find our true self, that does not mean there won't be opportunities to put that trauma back. We must be careful. For our minds remember what it was like to be that "fake self" and old habits may come up. It is our duty then to both recognize those old habits and let them go so that it does not recreate the thread when we are not paying attention, as well as to monitor ourselves as potential new trauma and threads arise, so that we don't create another wicked weave.

It is no easy process, but I find it to be a worthwhile one. People live their entire lives not knowing who they are as they are buried by the threads of trauma. It all begins with a single step, and it all continues by taking another single step. No need to rush. One step each day will carry us for miles.

Moments in Time

This next chapter is from an article that I've written about an encounter I've had with the threat of violence and I believe it to fit this book's theme very well. So the rest of this chapter will be that article.

I am writing this fresh off of an altercation that happened outside my martial arts school during class time. I am writing this as a way to document the experience for myself as well as make it public in case it might provide a learning experience for anyone else.

I was in the middle of instructing my Taiji class when we heard loud shouting from outside. We all look toward the door and start out to see what is going on as it wasn't the same kind of friendly shouts or drunken shouts that would be considered normal. As I looked out the door towards the shouting I saw two people starting a pushing match and there were a couple others attempting to talk sense into the both of them. I would later find out that these people were family to one of the people in the altercation. This is just happening a couple doors down from me and before I knew it my feet were already moving toward the people.

It was at this point that it was an almost out of body experience. I was watching my body move and though I was observing through my eyes, my body was moving on its own. As I was getting closer I saw what was a pushing match turned into something else as fists formed and punches started getting thrown. Seeing that, my pace quickened to a run. Before I knew it I stuck my hands between them and separated the two. In doing so I then stood between them. In the moments between seeing the first punch thrown and the moment I stood between them, about ten thousand possibilities flew through my head almost similar to the concept of one's life flashing before one's eyes. But those ten thousand things were almost like background noise as one thought remained the focus. "I must go."

I stood between them. Not thinking, but experiencing thought. I kept my eyes towards the middle in order to keep them both in my peripheral vision as I stood there. They continued to shout. There would be moments where they would both back off and moments they would try to reach each other. I knew at that moment that with their rising intention I had to relax and keep myself with a calm demeanor. In doing so I hoped to put water over the fire rather than feed the flames by also presenting myself with high intensity. Rather I sought to end the conflict without violence.

In time the police would arrive and I then let the police take over and handle the situation and I head back to finish teaching class. There was a lot to unpack as much happened in a short time. Ultimately looking back I was able to sort through a lot of the thoughts that raced through my mind as I was getting closer to the people. I was also able to see multiple things that I was trained in, practice, and now teach that came into play. In one sense I'm glad that the things I now preach are not just empty words, but something that has become very real through training.

After class I reflected on my ancestral altar. Each statue there depicts a character from mythology, history, and stories. And each one of those characters I put on the ancestral altar because they represent certain values. It is those values that I wish for those who come to my school to reflect on in themselves. Seeing those statues becomes a physical reminder of those values. In reflecting on the altercation, I got to see several of those values come into play.

(Guan Yu)

Guan Yu (the statue depicted in the photo) has many stories and I won't go into detail on those here, but essentially he was a famous Chinese general that was even believed to be a god of war. He wasn't a

143

general who would watch from the back, but he would lead from the front. So one of the values he represents is bravery.

In approaching the altercation, I had no idea what I was getting into. Their stature was not anything to write home about, but for all I knew, they could have been packing knives or firearms. It was one of the thoughts that flew by me as I approached. And though it is a scary thought looking back, I am still glad I got in between them. To me, the chance of stopping the conflict outweighed the possible dangers of something going wrong. And in that I am almost happy despite the poor situation that was happening as I didn't freeze up, but instead did what I was able to do to help. It is important to remember that bravery isn't lack of fear, but acting regardless of the fear.

(Lu dongbin)

Another character on my ancestral altar is Lu Dong Bin. He is depicted with a sword on his back. A very inconvenient place to have it as it would be more practical at the hip. This tells us though he can be capable of harm, he doesn't intend to harm at all. Thus he represents restraint. While the altercation after having stepped in lacked much need for restraint in terms of violence as things were starting to calm down, I found that keeping myself calm in hopes to not escalate things by having an intense demeanor was another type of restraint. Truthfully I found it to be a more difficult type of restraint as the intensity of the situation rises. It is easy to get caught up in it and follow the crowd as it were. Instead one must remain calm and hope your demeanor can affect theirs. Much like one positive person can change the vibe of a room filled with negativity.

(Guan Yin)

Lastly, Guan Yin, one of the three aspects of the Buddha represents compassion. Ultimately, compassion is the foundation of values. In witnessing this situation, I wanted to do my part to stop it as worse things could happen otherwise. Jumping into the fire of conflict in order to ensure the safety of those involved as well as those not involved. Compassion can manifest as bravery in one moment and restraint in another. At the end of the day, both of these people had a family. It was my wish for them both to see their families again. We can all come to understand this idea as most of us have that understanding. It is compassion that allows us to look past the surface of the situation which shows violence and anger, and instead see inside that both people suffer, both are just trying to live their day to day, both want to have dinner with their family.

I hope this writing of mine out of reflection is found to be useful. Peace be with you all.

Let Go of Your Mistakes

Not a single person on this earth is perfect. No matter how much one tries, they won't reach perfection in their lifetime. It makes one wonder why we spend so much time honing our craft. If we can never achieve perfection, why do we spend so much time on improving ourselves? Why not just settle. It is with such thoughts that one can bring up the often used saying, "It is not about the destination, but the journey to get there." Instead of focusing on some insurmountable goal, we live in the present moment to enjoy the toil of self-improvement. While the large goal may be far off, in the process of working towards it we may complete smaller goals and enjoy the fruits of said labor. This allows us to appreciate and enjoy the little things. Perhaps even come to understand that we don't have to be called for some great purpose that will somehow validate our existence.

Seeking validation is something many people look down on other people for as weak, yet don't realize that we all seek it to some degree. People will live their lives saying things like, "If I can just get this job, then I can support myself and make a name for myself. Then I will be happy." "If I can become a martial artist with a great reputation, then I will have made it." "If I can serve as some tool for god or some greater being, then my existence will mean something." All of us humans do this to some degree in some variant. We always look toward serving some higher purpose and we forget to live in the moment. Always looking forward, we will miss the beautiful sights if we don't stop to smell the flowers.

In coming to understand that this need for validation is present in all of us, we can forgive ourselves for it, but we must also work towards letting it go. Not getting angry at ourselves and working towards improvement. If one wants to work towards a larger goal, it is admirable and they should do it. However they should not live for the goal. If they live for nothing but the goal, then they have missed the point. Sometimes one should remember that they ultimately don't need validation. Living for the sake of living itself is just fine. Admirable even. It is okay for one to just live. No reason, no pomp or circumstance. Just live.

Along the path we travel, it is inevitable that we will trip over rocks, fall into pits, stray from the path. This is simply how life goes. It is important to pick ourselves back up, reorient ourselves, and continue to walk the path. We'll call these traps mistakes or failures. No human can escape failure. It comes with the territory of being imperfect. So why as humans are we so hard on ourselves? We fail our martial arts test or lose at sparring. We failed to get the job we wanted. We fail to make a pizza and now we have this inedible mess. It happens, yet many of us are hard on ourselves when it happens. Perhaps some will think if we are hard on ourselves, we won't make mistakes in the future. Or maybe they wish to punish themselves out of self-loathing. Many think of failure as some sort of negative thing, but actually without failure, we can never know true success.

Say we are born to a rich and successful family. We are born into success already. We grow up never knowing failure. So when we go out on our own for the first time and fail for the first time, it hits us hard. Having only tasted sweet, the bitterness becomes overwhelming. Now take a man born to poverty. Such a man born to failure may work hard to achieve greatness. Through trial and error they eventually find success and become rich. Having tasted bitter, they can appreciate the new sweet taste. However the analogy doesn't end here, for neither of these people have found the way. The man born to poverty may have found financial success, but living in success for so long changes people. We all see how money changes people. People forget their upbringing as they now live lavishly. They lose the friends that helped them towards this success as they focus on their wealth and maintaining it. They may have been brought financial success, but they have failed as friends. No matter how successful we are, we also fail. It is a yin/yang cycle we cannot escape. Success turns to failure, failure transforms into success. The true evil is thinking that one of these is good and the other bad.

Many teachers call it investing in loss. When we win at sparring, we hardly learn anything. We learn we are better than someone else at that moment. It gives us a sense of validation that what we are doing works. It reinforces, not improves. In loss, we can look at how we lost, why we lost, how we can improve to not lose the same way again. "I didn't fail 1,000 times. The lightbulb was an invention with 1,000 steps." Thomas Edison. As we see, there is nothing wrong with loss and failure. In fact, it is as much a good thing as success is. For those of us who take our failures to heart and are hard on ourselves, forgive yourselves. It is all part of the process of self improvement. Forgive oneself, learn from the mistake, and let it go.

The true way is to not get upset or overly joyful about either success or failure. Both are a part of the same continuum. Two sides of the same coin. One creates the other, and both are natural parts of life. The more we focus on some greater goal, the easier it is to lose sight of this truth. Keeping track of the smaller goals, we can see the multitude of successes and failures that happen through life. We can see from this that they are indeed a continuum. However if one only focuses on some greater unachievable goal, all they will see is failure. Until they can achieve the unachievable, all they will see is their failures to achieve this unachievable task. From this they will get the wrong idea that failure is bad. Only tasting bitter, never getting to enjoy sweet. So we must let go of needing to be something and instead simply "be." Observing success and failure floating by like clouds, learning and observing, yet not attaching or chasing. Learning to enjoy both the sweet and the bitter. Remember that there doesn't need to be a reason to exist. We need not be perfect. We work, we improve ourselves, we enjoy our lives and the journey. It is okay to simply exist. No need for justification, just be.

Impermanence

The only constant in the world we know is that all things are impermanent. We must accept this as reality. We don't live forever, our treasured possession will eventually wear and crumble, we won't be in the same position forever. Much of human life is spent attaching to and chasing things. Attempting to keep things as they are. Returning to, "The good ol days." As children we gain our friend group. As we age, we may grow apart. Perhaps our interests are different now, or our lives have led us in different directions. Sometimes we may think back on these times. We may wish to go back. Sometimes this leads to regaining old friends. Sometimes it leads to learning things about your old friends that you wish could be unlearned. Sometimes it just doesn't quite work out. Attempting to reach out is not what holds us down, it is the attachment to an end result that may not be achievable.

The people we think others are in our head are not what those people are. Even people we know well. We don't live in their head. We can't know them. We don't know anything about them except for what we can observe or what they tell us. But even then, what we observe can just be our perspective which is colored towards how we experience reality, and what they tell us could be lies for them to hide behind. If we attach to this idea in our heads, we attach to some version of someone that never existed. In learning the truth, it could be debilitating. As our world comes crashing down in what we thought we knew.

We must learn to not attach to what we don't want to cause us suffering. Attachments cause suffering, and all things are impermanent. Which means it is not a matter of if something will cause us suffering, but when. This said, this all does not mean that we can't attach to things. Just that we must know we are going to suffer for it. There is nothing wrong with attaching to loved ones, but disagreements may happen and we may suffer for it, because we care about them and hurtful words are worse coming from loved ones.

We practice martial arts. We must understand that we aren't going to improve everyday. Some days are bad days. Some days we are not well. Some days we had a fluke. We must continue practicing every day. We may not improve everyday, but everyday we practice we move towards improvement. Sometimes in climbing the mountain we meet walls or plateaus. Don't be discouraged. While improvement is impermanent, so are these walls or plateaus. You won't be stuck forever if you keep going.

All things on this earth are impermanent. All things will eventually crumble or die. Situations will change. Attaching to things will cause us to suffer when these things happen, however focusing on this eventuality is another kind of attachment. If you are with your family thinking about the eventuality that they will pass on, then you aren't living in the present moment and thus not enjoying your time with them to the fullest. For the things we choose to attach to, enjoy them when you have them. Treasure that time with them. When they are gone, grieve, then work towards letting go. It is a natural part of life. Suffering is impermanent also. If we don't attach to our suffering, it will eventually pass. Keep walking my friend.

Martial Arts without a Mouth

  Now at the end of this book, we return to the beginning. This whole book and all this writing was inspired by one simple phrase. The very phrase I used as the title. The context started from a simple facebook post. My teacher had posted a picture of himself in a horse stance. My teacher likes playing with the different saturation settings on photos. It ended up in a black and white picture that because of the setting caused his mouth to be whited out of the photo. My Elder Kung Fu brother commented on the photo saying, "Kung Fu without a mouth." This Kung Fu brother of mine is a fantastic martial artist and a very wise man who also likes silly humor. What he wrote was likely only made as a joke. At first I took it as such, however I repeated the phrase to myself again and I suddenly saw more in it.

  There was a lot more wise meaning in what was really just a joke. This book I write on martial philosophy has a lot to do with removing ego and coming to understand reality from a non-biased perspective. Ego gets in the way of martial training and life in general. The more time we spend stroking it, the less time we are training and improving. And what is the mouth but a physical manifestation of the ego.

  While not all uses of the mouth are about ego, it gives us a great analogy. When in conversation, it is important to spend a lot of time listening. When it is our time to speak, we speak. When it is time to listen, we listen. When the other is speaking, it is rude to interrupt them. Attempting to speak over someone is essentially saying, "What I am saying is more important than what you are saying, and what you say doesn't have weight." We can see how the analogy fits.

If we only ever talk and never listen, then we never learn anything new. We never grow. We know what we know. We don't know what we don't know. From the perspective of an egotistical person, they know everything as they don't know what they don't know. Because they think they know, they will speak and not listen. They think they have the answers. Instead we should listen. From listening we learn. We hear each other's perspectives and see things in a new light. We must not be a person who thinks he knows everything surrounding himself with people of the same opinions creating an echo chamber of ego. But seek to expand, learn, listen, seek out others who see things differently. Learn from all around us and see all there is to learn.

So train your ears to hear. Train your brain to learn, and process. Train your eyes to see. Your nose to smell. Your hands to reach out, to feel and touch. Train your bellies to digest new info and training. Train your heart to yearn for the ever expanding universe containing the plethora of things to learn. Train your feet to walk the path and to move forward. Train your body to the utmost to work towards continual improvement and let us together practice Kung Fu without a mouth.